Contents

Text copyright © BRF 2014
Authors retain copyright in their own work

Published by
The Bible Reading Fellowship
15 The Chambers
Abingdon, OX14 3FE
United Kingdom
Tel: +44 (0)1865 319700
Email: enquiries@brf.org.uk
Website: www.brf.org.uk
BRF is a Registered Charity

ISBN 978 0 85746 097 4

First published 2014
10 9 8 7 6 5 4 3 2 1 0

All rights reserved

Acknowledgments
Scripture quotations taken from The Holy Bible, New International Version Copyright
(Anglicised edition) copyright © 1973, 1978, 1984, 2011 by Biblica (formerly International
Bible Society). Used by permission of Hodder & Stoughton Publishers, an Hachette UK
company. All rights reserved. 'NIV' is a registered trade mark of Biblica (formerly International
Bible Society). UK trademark number 1448790.

Scripture quotations taken from The Holy Bible, New International Version, copyright ©
1973, 1978, 1984 by Biblica (formerly International Bible Society), are used by permission
of Hodder & Stoughton, an Hachette UK company. All rights reserved. 'NIV' is a registered
trademark of Biblica (formerly International Bible Society). UK trademark number 1448790.

Scripture quotations taken from The New Revised Standard Version of the Bible, Anglicised
Edition, copyright © 1989, 1995 by the Division of Christian Education of the National
Council of the Churches of Christ in the USA, and are used by permission. All rights reserved.

Scripture quotations from THE MESSAGE. Copyright © by Eugene H. Peterson 1993, 1994, 1995.
Used by permission of NavPress Publishing Group.

Extracts from the Authorised Version of the Bible (The King James Bible), the rights in which
are vested in the Crown, are reproduced by permission of the Crown's patentee, Cambridge
University Press.

Scriptures quoted from the Good News Bible published by The Bible Societies/HarperCollins
Publishers Ltd, UK © American Bible Society 1966, 1971, 1976, 1992, used with permission.
Scripture quotations from The Revised Standard Version of the Bible are copyright © 1946,
1952, 1971 by the Division of Christian Education of the National Council of the Churches of
Christ in the United States of America, are used by permission. All rights reserved.

Extract from As a Child by Phil Steer, published by lulu.com, 2012

A catalogue record for this book is available from the British Library

Printed by Gutenberg Press, Tarxien, Malta

The Editor writes...

Welcome to *Quiet Spaces*.

After the bustle and busyness of Christmas and the New Year, you may be looking forward to some quiet spaces at the moment. We will soon be leaving behind the dark nights and the cold winter and the special cosy quietness inside that comes with the season, and heading towards summer and a different type of space and quiet. In this issue, after considering the theme of light, we begin to look towards Lent and Easter. Many churches celebrate Candlemas around 2 February as a time of leaving Christmas and the Incarnation and turning to face the Passion and the journey through Good Friday to Easter morning. It is also a time when Jesus' presentation in the temple is remembered.

In this issue of *Quiet Spaces* we have divided Lent into three sections, each taking a different approach to the season. As with all *Quiet Spaces* material, please use these sections as appropriate to you and your circumstances. You may find you linger longer in one section and pass quickly through another, so be open to following God's calling through this time. Lent can be a good time for setting new habits, and maybe this year you will be looking at how and when you pray.

After the emotional rollercoaster that is Holy Week, try pausing on Holy Saturday, sharing the disciples' grief in preparation for that most holy of nights between Easter eve and Easter morning when Christ rose from the dead. We don't know at what point during the night this happened, and I enjoy the mystery of not knowing exactly when. It happened silently; no crowds of angels or a large audience, no public declaration, simply a quiet time with Jesus, Father and Spirit, followed by the realisation by Jesus' followers that yesterday he was dead, and today he is alive. And so this night shares the honour, along with the night of Jesus' birth, as a holy night when God's work is done in secret, in the stillness, and is then shared with humanity.

We also offer you three fellow companions on the way: St Teresa of Avila, James, and Joseph; each very different, but with something unique to teach us and experiences to share. You may also have your own fellow

3

travellers to share the spiritual journey, whether that is in praying together or in sharing your stories and experiences.

And so, as you journey and as you rest over the coming months, may you find those spaces where you meet with God and allow his story and your story to become entwined.

Sally Smith

PS: We would love to hear your views about *Quiet Spaces*. Do email us at enquiries@brf.org.uk or write to us at BRF, using the address on page 2.

Writers in this issue

Janet Fletcher is Team Vicar in the Rectorial Benefice of Bangor. She has contributed to *Guidelines* Bible reading notes (BRF) and *Pathway to God* (SPCK, 2006). She offers spiritual direction and enjoys teaching groups in prayer, spirituality and faith, and leading Quiet Days and retreats.

Angela Ashwin is a writer and speaker on spirituality. She has written several books about prayer and life with God, including *Faith in the Fool: Risk and delight in the Christian adventure* (Darton, Longman & Todd, 2009) and *Woven into Prayer: A flexible pattern of daily prayer* (Canterbury Press Norwich, 2010). She and her husband live in Southwell, Nottinghamshire.

Tony Horsfall is a freelance trainer and retreat leader based in Yorkshire, with his own ministry, Charis Training. He is an elder of Ackworth Community Church and has written several books for BRF, including *Working from a Place of Rest* (2010), *Rhythms of Grace* (2012), and most recently *Servant Ministry* (2013).

Janet Lunt trained in music, composes, creates artwork and leads Quiet Days. She has designed several multisensory prayer trails, which have been used in Bristol, including in the cathedral, and beyond. With a colleague, she recently created a series of children's reflective corners for publication.

Bridget Hewitt lives in Northumberland. She is a wife, mother of grown-up sons, and daughter of elderly parents, all of which form the background to her involvement in spiritual direction and group work, travelling the spiritual journey alongside teenagers and adults. She has a Masters degree in Christian spirituality.

Sally Smith enjoys creating spaces that enable encounter with God through leading Quiet Days and creating prayer corners and stations. She has led prayer groups in her local church, works as a spiritual director and writes and produces education materials.

Dorinda Miller has been leading Quiet Days and retreats in the UK and overseas, across denominations, for many years. She is currently involved in running Staying in the Vine, a six-week course on prayer and spiritual disciplines, in Nottingham.

Claire Musters is a freelance writer and editor, mother of two, pastor's wife and school governor. Claire's desire is to help others draw closer to God through her writing, which focuses on marriage, parenting, worship and issues facing women today.

God's light in our lives

Janet Fletcher

Light in the beginning

During these two weeks we will explore the theme of light and seek to reflect on the various ways in which we 'see' and understand light within our lives. In the book of Genesis we read:

> *In the beginning when God created the heavens and the earth, the earth was a formless void and darkness covered the face of the deep, while a wind from God swept over the face of the waters. Then God said, 'Let there be light'; and there was light. And God saw that the light was good; and God separated the light from the darkness. God called the light Day, and the darkness he called Night.*
> GENESIS 1:1–5A, NRSV

At the very beginning of the Bible, and the biblical story of God's relationship with creation and with humanity, we find this separation of light and dark, and read that the light 'was good'. Images of light and dark are found throughout the Bible, and in John's Gospel we read of the Word made flesh: 'in him was life, and the life was the light of all people. The light shines in the darkness, and the darkness did not overcome it' (John 1:4–5).

Here we have both the physical light and darkness of creation and the spiritual light of Jesus overcoming the physical and spiritual 'darkness' of the world. The light is seen to be good—and of God—and so, by implication, the dark is seen as bad or evil. Perhaps neither light nor dark can be described quite so simply, or separated in such a way.

Where there is light, we can see all things clearly: the furniture in our house, the roads we drive or walk along, the scenery around us. In the darkness comes a distortion, and at times fear, as we cannot easily make out all that is before our eyes. Yet even in the light, our inner self can feel shrouded by darkness. When we are stressed, ill, bereaved, or have lost our sense of direction in life, we can struggle to 'see' the light of God's presence with us and in the wider world.

As we journey through the light, it is important to remember that the light has its flip side, the dark, which is never far away.

What is your understanding of the word 'light'?

Witnessing and serving

'You are the salt of the earth; but if salt has lost its taste, how can its saltiness be restored? It is no longer good for anything, but is thrown out and trampled under foot. You are the light of the world. A city built on a hill cannot be hid. No one after lighting a lamp puts it under the bushel basket, but on the lampstand, and it gives light to all in the house. In the same way, let your light shine before others, so that they may see your good works and give glory to your Father in heaven.'
MATTHEW 5:13–16

These verses come after the Beatitudes and before other teaching by Jesus regarding our life in faith. They offer us insights into our witnessing and serving through the images of salt and light.

Salt enhances the taste of a dish; without it, the food prepared may seem bland and lacking in flavour. The salt allows the flavour to be revealed. Too much salt and a dish can be ruined and be harmful to our health. We need to find the right balance between too much and not enough.

The second image is light, a light that is not to be hidden away like a lamp placed under a 'bushel basket'. Jesus says that by placing a light on a lampstand it then gives light to all.

Salt and light, witnessing and serving, go together. At times we all feel unwell or tired, under pressure from work and home commitments, and so the salt and the light may become less flavoursome, less bright than we would like. Jesus' teaching on salt and light is for us all, in all the varied circumstances of our lives.

Take time to ponder salt and light.

Is the 'taste', the flavour of faith, still strong and vibrant for you?

Is the light of your faith lit in such a way that it can be seen by others?

Let my light shine

Let my light shine, O God, the light of faith and love for all, and for all creation.
In my stumbling steps along this pilgrim path of faith, and in my searching for all you ask of me, and desire in and for my life:

Be the Light I need in my life, the Light to guide my way.

In my concerns about the world, its need of a true and lasting peace, of the striving for justice and equality:

Be the Light I need in my life, the Light to guide my way.

6–19 JANUARY

In my relationships with family, friends and colleagues,
may the knowledge of your love inspire me to seek peace,
acceptance, reconciliation, care and hope to all I know:

Be the Light I need in my life, the Light to guide my way.

In my prayer and worship, may my heart be open to your love,
to your call, and be calm and still in your presence:

Be the Light I need in my life, the Light to guide my way.

Let my light shine, O God, the light of faith and love for all
people, and for all creation.

Candlelight and shade

Find a place where you can rest in comfort and quietness for prayer
and meditation. Bring with you a candle, large or small, to use as a
focus for prayer.

Light the candle.

Spend a little time becoming still within.

Close your eyes and ask God to be with you. Slowly imagine the
warmth of the candle flame, the warmth of God's peace and love
flowing through your body, beginning at the top of the head and slowly
journeying through the body, ending with the toes.

Open your eyes.

Look at the candle flame.

Take time to rest upon its colour, its movement, the light it offers, the
shades left where the light cannot quite reach.

When you are ready, bring into prayer the areas of light and shade
you find within.

10

What is your inner light—all you enjoy, all those you know and love?

What is to be found in the shade—all that is hidden and in need of cleansing, of forgiveness, of God's light?

Take as much or as little time in prayer as you feel is right for you.

As you draw the prayer to a close, reflect on all that has been prayed, giving thanks to God and making a note of anything you felt was significant.

Blow out the candle in the knowledge that Jesus is the light for all people, a light that the darkness cannot overcome (John 1:4–5).

The light of faith

Do you remember how you came to faith?

Do you remember how and when you first realised that Christ is 'the way, and the truth, and the life' (John 14:6)?

Do you remember who guided, supported, encouraged or influenced your path to the light of God?

The light of faith will no doubt have touched each one of us in different ways. The Spirit of God brings the light of faith to us in the way that each one of us, in our uniqueness, will be able to feel and respond to. The time we take to respond to the light of God's call may, of course, vary. For some, it may be sudden, perhaps even unexpected at that particular moment. For others, it may be a light that was shining around and within us for a long time, and that grew into a deeper personal realisation of all that God means in life and the way it is lived.

Does it matter how we come to the light of faith? We hope the answer is no. What does matter is what we do once the light of faith has been lit within our lives and how we bring God into the heart of our life.

If you have come to faith recently, it can be helpful to reflect upon the changes it has made to your life, the decisions you make, and your involvement with the wider Christian community.

If your spiritual journey has been one that could be described as being a 'slow, always with you' movement towards a deeper understanding of God, again it can be helpful to reflect upon how God shines into your life, the decisions you make, and your involvement within the wider Christian community.

It can be surprising, as we look back over our journey of faith, to discover the times and places when the light of God has revealed itself to us.

Colours of light

Wherever we go, colour is all around us. As the light moves over the land, the colours in the landscape change before our eyes, revealing shapes and hues not otherwise seen. There is a continual movement as the light plays with the painting of creation. The changing effect of light reveals something new to our eyes, and through our eyes, to our minds and hearts.

Living in Bangor, I see each day the way the light touches the contours of the mountains. The colours change with the movement of the sun, rain and clouds passing across them. It reveals, too, thoughts of wonder, awe, majesty, beauty, wilderness and danger.

If there is somewhere you can sit, looking at the landscape—mountains or fields, your local park, your garden, the sea shore or local rooftops—take time to sit quietly, and prayerfully reflect upon all you see. Look at the colours, the ways in which the light and shade touch the landscape and reveal new shapes or hues. Reflect too on the beauty and wildness, and upon God's presence in that place and his presence with you. What thoughts and images come to mind? When you leave, what do you take with you from that place?

Another approach to creative prayer is to gather a large piece of paper and crayons or paints. In a time of prayer, choose three or four colours and use those to draw, to make marks on the paper or let paint simply be 'thrown' randomly. You may wish to bring the colours together, to mix them or weave them one into the other. This is not the making of a masterpiece but allowing your inner thoughts to guide your hand on the paper. Reflect on why you chose the colours you did and upon all you see before you. What does it reveal about yourself and about God?

The hidden light within

How do you see yourself and how would you describe the essence of who you are? Alongside this question, there comes another: how do others see you and how would the people who know you describe the essence of who you are? As we discover and seek to understand 'who I am', we discover too something of our giftedness and the hidden light within us.

> *For now we see in a mirror, dimly, but then we will see face to face. Now I know only in part; then I will know fully, even as I have been fully known.*
> 1 CORINTHIANS 13:12

This verse is taken from the well-known passage on love, often read at weddings, as it speaks of love that never ends (v. 8). It speaks too, as in verse 12, of the God who is love, and in that love knows us fully. With God we stand in the light where all is seen and all is known and nothing is hidden.

At a time and in a place where you can be quiet and still, spend a little time reflecting in prayer upon the hidden light within; upon all that is illuminated and revealed, and all that has been placed in the dimly lit and seldom visited inner crevices.

Have a large piece of paper with you and divide it into three columns.

In the first column, write down all those things within that you feel have been hidden away and need to be acknowledged, and those things you know you are not good at.

In the second column, write down all the things you may attempt to do, or would like to try, but for which you would need some help and guidance.

In the third column, write down all those things that you know you can do, and all those things that you enjoy doing.

Take time to ponder all that has been written in each of the columns. Be gentle with yourself when looking at the first column. Be challenged to try something new, perhaps, from the second column. Be honest with yourself in how much from the third column you can offer, or already are offering, in God's service.

What is your hidden light within? What does this tell you about who you are?

Clouds play with the light

Your Light shines deep within my heart, O God,
it brings truth and hope, a way to follow, and yet,
the clouds come and go, and play with the light,
your light, bringing inner doubts and anxieties
to rise up, seeking a way out of that shaded cover.
The clouds play with my heart, tempting, O God,
leading astray my steps, and yet,
I seek the open way of your Light,
your forgiveness, your love.
At times, O God, the play of the clouds
obscures from the view
the challenges and changes to be faced,
of something necessary, for the good,
and as the clouds return to play behind the light once more,

there is clarity, and purpose and meaning,
as the veil is removed from the mind
and the heart, and all becomes clear.
Be with me, O God, in the clouds that play,
be with me, O God, in the joy of the Light,
be with me, O God, as I seek and desire, always
the Light of your way.
Amen

Reflection on John 8:12

Again, Jesus spoke to them, saying, 'I am the light of the world. Whoever follows me will never walk in darkness but will have the light of life.'

How did those listening react to these words? Jesus, strongly associating himself with God—'I AM'—must have made them wonder even more, 'Who is this?' Perhaps their thoughts took them back to the scriptures and the writing of Isaiah: 'The people who walked in darkness have seen a great light; those who lived in a land of deep darkness—on them light has shined' (9:2).

Biblically, darkness refers to night-time but also to the temptations and evils we face in the world, and so to a 'darkness' we all encounter in our lives. The light, therefore, which sustains even in the dark times, comes from following the One who is the light of the world. In Jesus we find a light to guide us, and also a life in which we can find wholeness, purpose and meaning. The light Jesus brings is one of love and compassion.

This verse always reminds me of the painting *The Light of the World* by Holman Hunt. Jesus is standing by a door with a lantern in his hand, and weeds and plants grow up the door, which has no handle. The door has to be opened from the inside. To walk in the light of life means that we make a choice: the choice to open the door—or not—and to step out into the world, bringing to it the light that shines out from us.

Dawn and sunset

To be prayed at the beginning or end of the day, as appropriate.

God of the dawn,
may your peace hover over this new day,
and may the freshness of this new day bring hope and possi-
bility of all that may be:

For with you is the fountain of life; in your light I see light.
(Psalm 36:9, changing 'we' to 'I')

God of the dawn,
may your love rise with the morning sun,
bringing to all creation the warmth of your presence.
In this day's new beginning,
may I seek to share the love you give to me with those I meet
this day:

For with you is the fountain of life; in your light I see light.

God of the dawn,
may your Light be my guide to enlighten my way,
my thoughts, my conversations, my work, my leisure, my
prayer this day:

For with you is the fountain of life; in your light I see light.

God of the dawn,
may your coming anew this day
enable me to face changes and challenges,
so I may give witness to Christ your Son.
As the sun rises to its peak, may its light be the true illumina-
tion I need for this day.

Amen

God of the sunset,
I lift to you this day, all that has been lived through and expe-
rienced.
Forgive me any times when I have neglected to be true to you,
or have ignored new possibilities for my life:

For with you is the fountain of life; in your light I see light.

God of the sunset,
your love remains as the day's sun begins to fade;
may the memories of all that has been good this day
sustain me through the night's darkening hours:

For with you is the fountain of life; in your light I see light.

God of the sunset,
be present in this evening time,
and may I be faithful to you in my times of rest,
in time spent with family, with friends or alone,
for I know your light still shines brightly within me:

For with you is the fountain of life; in your light I see light.

God of the sunset,
as the light of the sun is replaced by the light of the moon,
be with me and those I know and love
through the long hours of the night, and bring me,
renewed once more, to a new dawn and a new day:

Amen

Seeing the light in others

As a relationship deepens and grows, we begin to reveal more and more about ourselves; and as we do this we learn more about ourselves. As our relationship with God deepens and grows, we discover, too, something more of God present in our lives, and our need for God; and so again we learn more about ourselves.

Taking the time prayerfully to discover more about ourselves and about God, for our own personal journey of faith, reveals to us the movement of the Spirit in our lives. As we begin to recognise the feel and touch of God's light for ourselves, we will begin to see God's light in others.

In this light, we are called to be holy as God is holy, to seek harmony and peace, to offer welcome and hospitality, and to enable others to seek out the light of truth and faith. As we search for and discover this as a way of living, this influences the way in which we then relate to the rest of the world around us. To seek and desire to look inwards, and outwards, with the eyes of God, we will begin to see the light of love and goodness that shines out from others around us.

Think about the people you know (family, friends, colleagues, church members) and how God's light may be revealed through them. Is there someone you know whose faith has touched your life, bringing a deeper awareness of God, and so brought enlightenment to you?

Joy that lights up your life

Over these two weeks we have looked at light in many ways through the Bible, through prayer, through creation and the people we know as well as through the images of shade and cloud. We have the contrast of light with dark, a theme seen in the pages of John's Gospel.

Dark can be described using many colours, from navy to olive green, from grey to black, but when it comes to describing light in colours, it seems to be a little harder. White or yellow, perhaps, or maybe light is best described as being colourless or transparent. The darkness hides and obscures while the light reveals and makes clear.

What aspect of light—and shade—has touched you in some way? And why?

What brings a deep sense of joy to you and lights up your life?

Praying with St Teresa of Avila

Angela Ashwin

Teresa of Avila—friend of God

> Jesus said, 'I do not call you servants any longer, because the servant does not know what the master is doing; but I have called you friends, because I have made known to you everything that I have heard from my Father. You did not choose me but I chose you.'
> JOHN 15:15–16a, NRSV

It was a turning point in the life of St Teresa of Avila (1515–82) when she realised that her relationship with God could best be understood in terms of friendship. This great woman of prayer had already been a nun for about 20 years, mostly in the Carmelite Convent of the Incarnation. But she had constantly struggled with spiritual aridity in an environment where outward religious observance was emphasised and the inner life largely neglected. One day, however, everything changed while she was praying before a figure of the bound and scourged Christ. Profoundly moved by Christ's suffering, she experienced what she called her 'second conversion' and rededicated herself to his service. From now on her prayer would deepen and an intimate love relationship with God would continue to grow at the core of her being, becoming the wellspring of everything she did.

In her autobiography, known as the *Life* (translated and edited by E. Allison Peers, in *The Complete Works of Saint Teresa of Jesus*, Sheed & Ward, 1950), Teresa explains that she now had a deep and constant sense of God's presence and guidance, sometimes with visions and raptures which may seem strange to us. But at the heart of it all was her fundamental desire to be one with Jesus, to 'abide in him' and to allow him to dwell in her (see John 15:1–4).

You may like to return to the Bible verses mentioned above and respond to Jesus' loving invitation in whatever way feels right for you.

Images of prayer: watering the garden

Ho, everyone who thirsts, come to the waters.
ISAIAH 55:1a

In her new-found understanding of prayer as friendship with God, Teresa saw that our spiritual journey can be likened to watering the garden of our soul. In her *Life*, Chapter XI, she describes four ways in which a gardener might irrigate the land, identifying in each example elements that can apply to our own experience. We could be in any of these types of prayer at any particular time, and God's living water is always available to us, no matter what we are experiencing.

Her first image is of the gardener trudging backwards and forwards with a bucket. This is laborious work, and not always satisfying because sometimes the well seems to have run dry. Our prayer, says Teresa, can feel like this. We find that we have to work hard at it and we easily become discouraged, especially if our efforts seem to produce nothing but spiritual dryness. But her message is clear: trust God and don't give up! What matters most is not how our prayer happens to feel but how faithful we are in persevering. Even when the well of our spiritual life *appears* to be drying up, the truth is that God will never fail or abandon us.

If we keep going when our experience of prayer is barren, we learn to surrender ourselves to God in sheer trust, depending less on good feelings during our devotions. Our offering of prayer is all the more valuable when we are simply carrying on in faith and there is apparently little in it for us. In the end, by staying open and loving towards God, we are likely to discover, like Teresa, how deeply we have been loved and held by God all along.

Have you ever experienced dryness in your prayer life? Does the image of watering the parched earth in a garden speak to you? A dried-up potted plant on the windowsill can also be a powerful image. You might like to pray: 'Lord, come into my thirsty soul like water into a dry plant.'

Images of prayer: the water-wheel or 'windlass'

All Teresa's images of prayer are designed to encourage us rather than to make us feel that we are failing if we never get beyond the 'bucket' stage. She often reminds her readers that, whenever we pray and whatever form our prayer takes, God is at work anyway.

In Teresa's second example of watering the land (*Life*, XIV–XV), the gardener uses a 'windlass' (a device driven by a crank winding a rope round a drum), so that less effort is now required. Similarly, she suggests, we begin to find that we do not have to work so hard when we pray, because our prayer does not depend just on us. The grace of God is active with us and in us, sometimes in spite of ourselves, so we can spend time resting in God, allowing ourselves to be still and quiet instead of being continually at work.

The apostle Paul would probably have agreed. He himself often laboured over his prayers, but discovered that his primary task was simply to rely on God: 'Therefore, to keep me from being too elated, a thorn was given to me in the flesh, a messenger of Satan to torment me, to keep me from being too elated. Three times I appealed to the Lord about this, that it would leave me, but he said to me, "My grace is sufficient for you, for power is made perfect in weakness." So, I will boast all the more gladly of my weaknesses, so that the power of Christ may dwell in me' (2 Corinthians 12:7b–9).

Are there aspects of your prayer that feel empty or seem to involve a lot of effort? It is worth pondering why this is so. It may be that you are trying to pray in a way that is no longer suitable for you. Sometimes, of course, hard work in prayer is good, such as when we give ourselves to intercession or persevere with a pattern of praying that we know holds us close to God, even if it does not always feel particularly good. Whatever way of praying you find best at the moment, allow yourself some moments when you do not say or do anything other than resting in God's love and healing presence.

Images of prayer: the stream

As a deer longs for flowing streams, so my soul longs for you, O God.
PSALM 42:1

Teresa now moves into a further aspect of prayer where we are more receptive than active as God's transforming love flows through our being. She likens this to a spring or stream watering a garden at a deep level without the gardener having to do very much at all. This is not an experience that we can engineer; it is a gift, freely bestowed on us by God when the moment is right.

Spend some time reflecting on your own spiritual journey, seeing if there have been any times when you have known God's presence with you, without your having to do or say anything much. Sometimes people experience a great calm or a sense of mystery and awe during church worship, so that they know themselves to be held in the divine love. This can also happen when we are in places of natural beauty, as well as during a time of prayer. It is as if the 'Martha' side of us, always busy and doing things for God, is now giving way to the 'Mary' side, so that we are content simply to be present, open and attentive before God (see Jesus' visit to the house of Martha and Mary, Luke 10:38–42). Later, you may look back and realise that you have been receiving what Teresa sees as the sweet and delightful water of grace permeating your soul (see *Life*, XVI).

Images of prayer: the deluge

If you have ever stood outside during a heavy downpour, your face turned upwards, you will know how powerful the sheer force, sound and sensation of torrential rain can be. Such moments remind us how small we humans are when exposed to the mighty elements of creation.

Teresa uses this image in an attempt to describe an overwhelming experience of prayer. Just as the gardener does nothing but simply watches as the heavens open and saturate the earth, we may sometimes have a powerful moment of awareness of God that takes us by surprise and draws us into a different level of consciousness (*Life*, XVII). Teresa acknowledges that many people who pray never experience anything like this, and those who do cannot stand the intensity for long. We are not second-class Christians if our prayer life is more mundane than this, and we can still receive the abundance of divine love perfectly well in less spectacular ways. One of Teresa's aims in writing about this is to warn us against spiritual pride. If we should have an unusually strong experience of God, this is a gift and is happening only because we must be in need of it. It is never a sign of our imagined worthiness or holiness.

Teresa finds it helpful to describe prayer in terms of rain. What is your current image of prayer? Do any pictures or colours come to mind that convey something of your relationship with God? You could experiment with sketching, painting or using pastels or clay; these activities can themselves be a way of praying.

Teresa's courage and perseverance

'Do not let your hearts be troubled. Believe in God, believe also in me.'
JOHN 14:1

'Do not worry about tomorrow, for tomorrow will bring worries of its own. Today's trouble is enough for today.'
MATTHEW 6:34

These words of Jesus must have strengthened Teresa during many severe trials and setbacks. After the spiritual experience that she called her 'second conversion', she became certain that God was calling her to carry out a radical reform of the Carmelite order, which had slipped into lax and excessively comfortable ways. So she worked indefatigably to found reformed houses for sisters and also friars all over Spain, encountering considerable opposition in the process as well as huge practical and financial problems. But she continued undaunted, with a profound trust in the God who never let her down.

Her journeys were frequently hazardous as she and her companions bumped over rough and lonely terrain in simple carts, often in severe weather. An apocryphal story tells how they were crossing a ford one day when a donkey stumbled and all their possessions fell into the water. Teresa is said to have responded, 'Dear God! If this is how you treat your friends, no wonder you have so few of them!' Regardless of whether or not this actually happened, it captures well Teresa's robust and honest relationship with God. She kept going against all the odds, and her deep faith and courageous obedience can be an inspiration to us, especially if we are trying to cope with major difficulties or hurtful opposition.

The following words are also commonly attributed to Teresa. Though almost certainly not written by her, they do reflect her often-repeated conviction that the ultimate purpose of all our living and praying is love:

> *Christ has no body now on earth but yours.*
> *Yours are the eyes through which he looks*
> *with compassion on this world;*
> *yours are the feet with which he walks to do good;*
> *and yours are the hands with which he blesses others now.*
> ATTRIBUTED TO TERESA OF AVILA, EXACT SOURCE UNKNOWN

Are you able to say the following words to God?

> *Christ, you have no body now on earth but mine.*
> *Mine are the eyes through which you look*
> *with compassion on this world;*
> *mine are the feet with which you walk to do good;*
> *and mine are the hands with which you bless others now.*

How does it feel to use the words in this way? The good news is that we do not have to offer ourselves to Christ in our own strength. The grace of God comes to meet us as soon as we express our desire to serve others in Christ's name. Teresa herself tells us that she could not have kept going, nor could she have faced the great troubles in her life, without the grace of God constantly supporting her.

Teresa's bookmark

After Teresa's death in 1582, the nuns found a bookmark tucked into her breviary (her book of daily psalms, hymns, readings and prayers). On it she had written these words:

Nada te turbe,
Nada te espante,
Todo se pasa,
Dios no se muda.
La paciencia
Todo lo alcanza;
Quien a Dios tiene
Nada le falta;
Sólo Dios basta.

Let nothing disturb you,
Let nothing frighten you,
All things pass
But God never changes.
Patience
Achieves everything;
Whoever has God
Lacks for nothing;
God alone suffices.

You might like to make your own bookmark with these words, perhaps scribing the text yourself, or photocopying this page on to a card.

Teresa's *Interior Castle*: problems and forgiveness

'In my Father's house there are many dwelling places. If it were not so, would I have told you that I go to prepare a place for you?'
JOHN 14:2

'But whenever you pray, go into your room and shut the door and pray to your Father who is in secret; and your Father who sees in secret will reward you.'
MATTHEW 6:6

When Teresa was 62 years old, exhausted by constant travelling and vilified by those who were trying to undermine her reforms, she responded to a request from a priest who supported her that she should make a written account of her understanding of prayer. Incredibly in such circumstances, she produced a spiritual masterpiece, *The Interior Castle* (translated with commentary by Dennis J. Billy, C.Ss.R., Ave Maria Press, 2007). Here she describes our soul as a beautiful inner castle with many 'rooms' or 'mansions', representing different aspects of ourselves and of our prayer. God dwells in the seventh and innermost room, and the nearer one gets in prayer to the centre, the more dazzling the divine light becomes.

In her description of the outer three mansions of our soul, Teresa uses vivid imagery. Our faults, errors and petty distractions are like reptiles and other nasty creatures, she says, that block us off (at least partly) from the divine light. We need to acknowledge our failings and receive forgiveness in order to grow closer to God. But the wonderful thing about Teresa's castle is that every wall is transparent, made of crystal glass, so the divine light can penetrate even to the darkest parts of our psyche. There is nowhere in our inmost being that God cannot reach if we are willing to turn our face towards his cleansing and healing light.

Do conflicting desires, discouragements or neglect of prayer hinder your spiritual life? God's mercy pours out towards us all, like sunshine, as soon as we acknowledge our failings and ask for forgiveness and a fresh start.

Teresa's *Interior Castle*: into stillness

Whenever you come back to your inner castle in your mind's eye, it can help to offer a prayer on these lines:

In trust and thankfulness I enter the quiet, welcoming space of my interior castle. Here I am alone with God, safe and loved. I open my heart and mind to receive the divine mercy and light that are coming to meet me. And I offer myself to be, with God's help, a channel of light and peace in the world.

In the fourth mansion of Teresa's *Interior Castle* there is more quietness and a stronger sense of the mystery of being with God. We use fewer words and discover that God is doing more while we are doing less. We are increasingly dependent on divine grace, with a greater trust in the God who is at work in and through us.

We probably still experience distractions as our chatterbox minds leap around, but we also find ourselves dipping into a level of prayer deeper than words. Teresa sees this as part of our ongoing friendship with God, who gently draws us back to himself again and again. No matter how many times we turn away or forget to pray, we can always return to our inner place of prayer. Teresa is clear that the doors of the castle are never locked, and as soon as we show even a glimmer of desire to pray once more and grow closer to God, we are inside! God never forces himself on us, but the invitation to renew this loving relationship of prayer is always open. Simply take a verse of scripture, recommends Teresa, and let it lead you back into the stillness of God's presence. Even if you have only five or ten minutes in a day, this practice is of infinite value.

Spend some time slowly mulling over these words:

Be still, and know that I am God!
PSALM 46:10a

Teresa's *Interior Castle*: the silkworm

Teresa uses the delightful image of the silkworm in her account of the fifth mansion, to show what happens when we abandon ourselves even more deeply into God's hands. Just as the silkworm starts life feeding on mulberry leaves, so we are nourished by worship, especially the Eucharist, and by meditating on scripture and other spiritual teachings. But then the worm spins a cocoon around itself and 'dies' to its former way of being. Similarly, says Teresa, we have to die to anything that makes us selfish, arrogant, greedy or unkind as we surrender ourselves to Christ. Here she quotes Paul's words in Colossians 3:3: 'For you have died, and your life is hidden with Christ in God.' This 'dying to self' is not a soul-destroying obligation, as if we had to make ourselves miserable in order to please God. On the contrary, when we let go of our ego or 'false self', we can find peace and fulfilment.

There may be times in our spiritual journey when we feel confused, even abandoned by God, like a silkworm helpless in its dark cocoon and undergoing radical changes. Teresa encourages us to persevere, trusting that we are being transformed in ways we may not understand but that will ultimately enable us to become more our true selves, the persons God created us to be—like a beautiful white butterfly or moth emerging from its chrysalis. Whenever our old ego is dissolved and transformed in the light of Christ, whether in large ways or small, we are growing spiritually. Our task is to remain open and ready for God to work in us.

Many children's books have an underlying message that we adults do well to hear. See if you can get hold of a copy of *The Very Hungry Caterpillar* (Eric Carle, Puffin Books, 2000). As you read it, enjoy its gentle humour, and pray for discernment as to how this story might be speaking to you.

Teresa's *Interior Castle*: the wax tablet

Another image used by Teresa in her fifth mansion is that of a wax tablet. When we pray, we are sometimes completely passive, she says, like a tablet in the hands of a scribe. This does not mean that we just sit back and stop bothering, or that we will emerge from every prayer time with a kind of divine text message. It is simply a matter of being present to God with our whole being, consenting to be used and guided as God wants.

Sometimes it helps to turn this image round and become the scribe ourselves as we write down our inmost thoughts and prayers in what is known as 'journalling'. What often happens, over time, is that we begin to discover new things about ourselves, our deepest desires and our relationship with God as we write.

Reflective journalling: write down what has spoken to you most during these days of prayer with Teresa of Avila. Note down in particular things that have helped you to pray, and anything you want to explore further. Then stop and be still and open before God, and imagine that you yourself are now a blank page or a wax tablet in the hands of God. Don't try to make anything happen or force a 'message' into your mind. Simply be available to God, putting yourself at his disposal.

Closing prayer:

O God, I place myself in your hands.
Do whatever you want with me;
inscribe your love in my soul.

Taking this further

Teresa's closing chapters about the interior mansion describe how God leads the soul into ever deeper union with himself. If you want to pursue this further, there are several helpful books about Teresa's Castle and its meaning for us (for example, Ruth Burrows, *Interior Castle Explored*, Sheed and Ward, 1981).

The following prayer is a paraphrase of some of Teresa's words in her autobiography and poems, especially her *Poem No. 2.*

Beloved God,
I am yours; I was born to serve you.
What is your will for me?

King of my life,
source of all wisdom,
kindness and gentleness,
I am your servant;
even with my faults and failings
I still sing of love for you.
What is your will for me?

You created and redeemed me,
you called me and loved me,
you waited patiently for me.
O my sweet Love,
show me where, how and when?

I am ready.
What is your will for me?

You might like to try the challenge of praying these words daily over a few weeks. It may be just an aspiration to begin with, something that you would *like* to be able to pray wholeheartedly. Some people find that when they use a prayer regularly in this way, they grow into it so that it becomes part of them. Teresa is a good guide to take with us as we continue to explore our friendship with God.

James: a faith that works

Tony Horsfall

An introduction to the letter of James

Martin Luther famously described the letter of James as an 'epistle of straw'. He felt that it had very little value for the church because it lacked doctrinal content and logical structure. Luther may have been right about many significant things, but I feel that he badly misjudged this little epistle. It is full of sound, practical advice and straight-talking wisdom, challenging us to express our faith in everyday life. That is a challenge that most of us need.

As far as James is concerned, true faith will be shown in our actions. If our faith has no outward expression, then it is dead. It is no good talking about helping others if we do nothing; we must actually do something to meet the needs around us (James 2:14–17). In particular, we must care for the poor and treat them with dignity and respect (2:1–11; 5:1–6).

A variety of other interesting topics are covered in the letter in the free-ranging style that characterises the writing of James: persevering through trials and temptations, responding to God's word, being careful in our speech, finding true wisdom, developing friendship with God, being patient in suffering, and learning to pray. Anyone looking for a manual on what it means to be a Christian in everyday life will find it here.

These notes are not intended to be an in-depth exposition of the epistle. Rather, the purpose is to help you to get a feel for what James has to say and to whet your appetite for more. Above all, my intention is that we should not only think about what we read, but internalise it so that it becomes part of us and determines how we behave. Over the next two weeks, then, listen carefully to God and seek to make a connection between your faith and your everyday life.

Facing trials

James 1:2–4, 12

Trials are those difficulties in life that challenge our faith and can potentially undermine our trust in God. It is important that we learn how to respond to difficulty, not in resignation, but in positive understanding of what God is doing in us, even through the hard times. James suggests five ways to respond to trials.

- Recognise that trials are normal: they come to everyone at some point. Some may be minor (the car breaks down, the bus is late), some major (someone gets cancer, we lose our job). Facing difficulty is simply part of life.
- When we face trials, our faith will be tested. We can find ourselves thinking either that God doesn't love us and has forsaken us, or that we have done something wrong and it's all our fault. Neither conclusion is justified. God does not guarantee us a pain-free life, and trials do not mean he has abandoned us or that he is punishing us.
- If we face trials with God's help, our faith will get stronger. Rather than giving up because things are hard, we will find new resources of strength and grace to keep going. In a word, we will learn to persevere. Perseverance is one of the most important qualities in the

life of any believer. It means that we stay faithful to God to the very end, even when times are tough.

- When, over the course of a lifetime, we show such perseverance, our faith will become mature or fully grown (adult). No longer will we exhibit 'baby' faith, demanding that God gives us everything we want and getting mad with him when he doesn't. Our faith will have become resilient, and even under severe trial we will know from experience that we can still trust God.
- Such faith is pleasing to God and expresses deep love. In the life to come it will be rewarded. Those who persevere will receive the crown of life.

A personal reflection

James 5:10–11

As a backdrop to this section, read James 5:10–11.

Think about your life at this moment. What kind of trials are you facing? Make a list. Would you describe them as 'minor' or 'major'?

What has been your response to them? Have you been tempted to doubt God's care? Have you been tempted to blame yourself?

How was Job an example of perseverance? How can his example, and what you have already read in James (1:2–4, 12), inspire you to keep going in your walk with God?

Invite God in his compassion and mercy to share these trials with you by imagining him there with the people and in the events. What is he saying or doing? Hold the scene and receive God's presence into those situations.

Why not share your thoughts and feelings with someone you know who will pray with you?

Listening well

James 1:19–21

I used to think that I was a good listener. After all, I had been a pastor for many years and often listened to people as they shared their concerns. I thought that listening was easy: it simply required me to stop talking! I'm embarrassed to admit it now, but that's the way I used to think.

The change came for me when I attended a course on listening skills and realised that I didn't actually listen at all—I simply waited for my turn to speak. In the interval between speaking and speaking again I was thinking what I would say next, not fully listening to the other person.

James here highlights a key skill that lies at the heart of all effective relationships: attentive listening. By this we mean concentrating fully on what the other person is saying, giving them our whole attention and really 'hearing' their words. This requires us to switch off temporarily from our own agenda and tune in to what is being said (or not said) by the other person. Only then will we truly receive what they are trying to communicate.

James puts it so well: 'Everyone should be quick to listen, slow to speak and slow to become angry' (1:19, NIV).

It may be worth reflecting on your own ability to listen. Rather than assuming that you are a good listener, assume that (like the majority of us) you are not. Then seek to practise listening to others. If you have not done so already, attend a course on listening skills (easily found through the internet). You will be amazed what a difference listening well will make to your relationships, whether at home, at work or at church.

When have you been truly listened to? How did it make you feel? What made you realise that the other person was really listening to you? Try to do the same for someone else. When you find yourself this week in conversation, listen rather than speak. Enquire sensitively about the other person's well-being without being intrusive. Give them plenty of time to speak. Listen carefully to what they say, and to the feelings behind their words. Let them know you care.

Mirror, mirror, on the wall

James 1:22–25

You will be familiar with the wicked queen in the story of Snow White, who used a mirror to convince herself of her own beauty. How disappointed she was when she realised that she was no longer the fairest of them all! She was annoyed when the mirror spoke the truth, but a mirror is always honest and reflects back only what is before it.

This is a meditation about mirrors. As a backdrop to it, read James 1:22–25 and have a mirror with you or place yourself in front of one.

Think about the mirrors in your house. How many do you have? Where are they positioned, and why? Do you have different kinds of mirrors and do they have different purposes? How do you use them? Do you take one with you when you are travelling? Could you manage without a mirror, or not at all? What is the purpose of having a mirror?

Now, as you look in the mirror before you, what does it tell you?

James says that the word of God is like a mirror. Why do you think he makes this comparison?

Now, imagine yourself getting ready for an important function, and looking in the mirror before you leave. You notice that your hair is untidy or your tie isn't straight. What do you do? Do you take no notice and walk away or do you stop and make an adjustment?

James says that when we allow the word of God to correct us like this, and when we adjust our behaviour accordingly, then we will know the blessing of God upon our lives. This is how we become self-aware and how we are changed into the likeness of Christ.

Can you think of a time when God challenged you through his word to change your behaviour or attitude? How did you respond? Did you find it hard to be corrected? If so, why was that? Did you make an adjustment? If so, what helped you to obey?

As you look in the mirror, pray that God will help you to be honest with yourself, and to see yourself as God sees you—both in challenging you to change and also in accepting the good about yourself.

Look in the mirror again. See yourself as God sees you. What does he see? He loves what he sees, so recognise his love and receive it. What in particular does he love? Yes, we fall short of what God wants for us, but he loves us nonetheless. Ask God how you can become more fully the child he made you to be.

Spotlight on Richard Stearns

Richard Stearns had a successful career as CEO of an American tableware company. Married with five children, he lived in a large house, drove a Jaguar and travelled widely, always first class and staying in the best hotels. Respected in his community, influential in his large suburban church and generous in his charitable giving, he was the epitome of a 'successful' Christian. Or so he thought.

Out of the blue he was invited to become President of World Vision, a Christian organisation dedicated to working with families and children, and to tackling the causes of poverty and injustice. He felt inadequate and unqualified for such a role, and resisted the opportunity until God showed him without any shadow of a doubt that this was the job for him.

The move meant a change of location for his family and a huge drop in salary, but more significant was the impact it had on his faith.

His first trip abroad, to Uganda, completely took him apart when he saw first-hand the suffering of AIDS victims, especially the children. Overwhelmed by what he encountered, his tears began to flow. Right there and then he prayed that God would forgive him for his ignorance of the effects of poverty—and yet, by his own admission, he wasn't ignorant at all.

Like many of us, he knew well enough about poverty and suffering in the world. He was aware that children die daily from starvation and lack of clean water. He also knew about AIDS and the orphans it leaves behind, but he chose to keep these things outside of his insulating bubble and look the other way. This was to be a moment that would ever after define him. His sadness that day was replaced by repentance. Despite what the Bible had told him so clearly, he had turned a blind eye to the poor.

You can read about the encounter Richard Stearns had with God in Uganda, and his work for World Vision, in his book *The Hole in Our Gospel* (Thomas Nelson, 2009). He recognised that something was missing from the way he had been expressing his faith, and he determined to put it right. It is a challenging read, because many of us also have a 'hole' in our gospel.

During the coming week, be aware of news stories in the media that bring home to you the plight of the poor, whether overseas or in your own locality. Pray that God will burst the bubble of your own insensitivity to their need and give you a heart of compassion. Think about how you can respond; in prayer, by giving, through actions. Do something tangible to show you care.

No favouritism

James 2:1–4

As a background to this imaginative meditation, read James 2:1–4. Here we are invited to 'suppose' (that is, imagine) a particular scenario that happens in a local congregation. Imagine you are on welcome duty when two visitors arrive, and try to place yourself in the scene that morning.

There you are standing at the door to greet people. How do you understand your 'job description'? Is it an important task? How do you feel about this role? Is it something you enjoy doing or not?

The first to arrive is the rich man. Try to imagine his appearance, complete with gold ring and fine clothes. What is your first impression? How do you greet him? Notice what is going on inside you as well as how you treat him. Do you show him to a seat? Where do you suggest he sits? What do you say as you leave him there?

Next comes someone very different. He is obviously poor and will be needy in other ways. Try to imagine his appearance, dressed as he is in shabby clothes, unkempt, lacking in personal hygiene. What is your first impression? What is happening inside you? What are you thinking and feeling? Do you show him to a seat? Where do you suggest he sits? What do you say to him? What does your tone of voice reveal?

Reflect on the way you responded to each visitor. How do you think Jesus might have handled this situation? Would this change the way you welcome people in future?

James says that there should be no favouritism amongst the followers of Jesus. Why is this so? How does this exercise help you to get in touch with your own feelings about unfair treatment, even in church? How might your own behaviour be affected by these thoughts?

Creative time

The book of James uses a lot of helpful imagery taken from the world around us. Read the following passages. Which do you feel drawn to? Use it as an inspiration for painting, modelling or creative writing. As you work, be aware of how this reflects your life and allow God to show where he is in the scene. You may like to read around the verses given to discover the context.

1:6: like a wave of the sea, blown and tossed by the wind.
1:10: like a wild flower, fading beneath a scorching sun.
3:5: like a forest fire, set ablaze by a single spark.
3:11: like a spring, pouring out both fresh water and brackish.
4:14: like a mist that appears briefly and then vanishes.
5:7: like a farmer, waiting for the rain to come.

Taming the tongue

James 3:1–12

James makes several references to the tongue in his epistle, but it is only here that he develops the theme in detail, graphically portraying the trouble that can arise through careless talk. Believers should be gracious in their speech, and wholesome words can have a positive effect. James, however, suggests that our words may well let us down.

• Verses 1–2: our speech betrays our sinfulness most easily, for all of us make mistakes in what we say, and none is without fault. That is why those who teach in church, or use words for a living, must be most careful of all, because their words can either blister or bless; they can hurt or they can heal. We will all give account to God for

43

our words and in particular those who are called to speak on behalf of God.

- Verses 3–5: the tongue is only a tiny part in the body, yet it wields a great influence. A small bit can guide a mighty horse. A small rudder can steer a great vessel. A small spark can start a forest fire, and as James so rightly says, 'the tongue also is a fire' (v. 6). Careless and uncontrolled words can wreak havoc in relationships and destroy harmony between people. Gossip, backbiting and malicious talk escalate a conflict and divide friends.
- Verse 6: of course the fuel of such a fire comes essentially from hell itself, because the devil loves to stir up conflict, arouse the passion of anger and push people into intemperate extremes in their words and actions, usually without them even realising what is happening.
- Verses 7–8: in the light of this, we must all recognise our helplessness. We can tame all kinds of animals but not the tongue; we can conquer outer space but not our passions. We need outside help, help that only God can give.
- Verses 9–12: what we need to see is the inconsistency between our beliefs and our behaviour, between who we are and what we do. It should be inconceivable that one moment we praise God and the next minute we berate our neighbour. If we have become children of God, then we share his divine nature and have his life within us. The 'stream' of words that flows out of us should reflect this and be of pure, fresh water (life-giving), not bitter or salty (bringing sickness and death). The 'fruit' of our lips should be consistent with our standing in Christ, not a strange contradiction.

Only as we grow more fully into our identity as God's children can we hope to tame the tongue; only as we begin to live according to our new identity will we see a difference in our speech.

For thought: as you ponder this passage, what challenges you the most? What do you feel God wants to say to you about your speech? How do you feel about this? What hope does James give us that we can change? Turn your thoughts and feelings into prayer, perhaps writing down what you want to say.

A review of the day

The prayer of Examen is a way of helping us to reflect on how we are living and to see how God has been at work in our lives. With the help of the Holy Spirit, we are invited to think back over the day that is just ending and to remind ourselves of what happened. For this particular exercise we will use the Examen to consider words that have been spoken.

Think back over the day since you first woke up. What was the first word you spoke and to whom? And what was the first thing said to you and by whom?

As you think about the day, what significant conversations did you have?

How do you feel about your own words in the course of the day? What did you say that was helpful? Were you able to speak words of encouragement, healing or hope? If so, give thanks to God.

Did you speak words that you now regret or with hindsight feel were unhelpful? Ask for, and receive, God's free and full forgiveness. Consider if you might want to say sorry to someone tomorrow for a careless word today.

What have you learned about your speech today? Pray that God will help you in all your conversations tomorrow, giving you the words to say and helping you to guard your tongue. Follow this exercise every day for a week, and see what difference it makes to your speech.

Two kinds of wisdom

James 3:13–18

Wisdom can be defined as the ability to make good decisions. Even intelligent, well-informed people don't always have wisdom when it comes to making decisions about life and relationships, and some who are otherwise regarded as successful can make poor choices when it comes to their own conduct and behaviour.

According to James, the key to receiving wisdom for life is to acknowledge our lack of it, and to ask God to supply it (1:5). This kind of wisdom 'comes from heaven' (3:17) and is a gift, not simply the product of human intelligence or reasoning.

Such wisdom is easily recognised because it is expressed in humility and by the way one lives. Those for whom wisdom has become a way of life will approach situations and decision-making in a certain manner (17–18). They are characterised by pure motives, wanting what is right. They seek a peaceful outcome, doing their best to understand other points of views, to be cooperative and compassionate, and to demonstrate the fruit of the Spirit. They seek to be non-judgmental and free of prejudice, and above all to approach things with honesty and sincerity. Such people create an atmosphere of peacefulness and open the way for good decision-making and the unity that follows.

However, there are others whose hearts are not so pure (14–16). They are motivated by envy and rivalry on the one hand, and personal ambition on the other. Once these toxins have entered the stream of decision-making, it is sure to be polluted. Such people may generate plausible-sounding reasons for what they are doing, but this is not God's wisdom. Rather, it is 'earthly' in its origins, the product of human pride and lacking in real spiritual values. Indeed, it creates all kinds of division and unhelpful behaviour, and may even be intensified by the devil's interference, who likes nothing more than to divide God's people.

Each of us has the responsibility to make sure that we are living according to God's wisdom, not our own, and to ask for his wisdom in all our personal decisions. Likewise, when we are making decisions together with others, it is vital that we cleanse our hearts of any attitudes and approaches that could send our deliberations 'off course'. Time spent in prayer expressing our dependency on God and putting our hearts right before him will reap great rewards.

What can you learn from this about your personal decision-making?

What decisions have you made today, whether large (for example, to change jobs) or small (what to have for lunch)? How did your faith inform those decisions?

As you think about future decisions you have to make, how can you apply the teaching of James?

Prayers for wisdom

For personal discernment:

Lord, I come before you in my need,
recognising my dependency upon you,
asking for wisdom and guidance.
Forgive me for my self-will
and tendency to determine my own future.
Place in my heart the desire to do your will;
plant in my mind an understanding of your ways;
guide my feet into the path of peace;
and grant me the grace to follow fully.
This I ask that your name may be glorified in my life. Amen

For group discernment:

We pause, O Lord, at the start of our meeting
to seek your face and to ask for your direction.
We confess our tendency to want to rule our own lives
and to have things our own way.
We acknowledge that within each of us there lie dormant
such things as envy and rivalry, pride and selfish ambition.
Wash us and cleanse us, O God, before ever we begin to discuss holy things;
deliver us from any attitude, presupposition or prejudice that may be a hindrance to our discerning your will together.

(Pause)
And now, gracious Lord, fill us afresh with the Spirit of wisdom and revelation
in the knowledge of Jesus Christ, that we may know him better.
Grant us to listen attentively, both to one another and to you,
with openness, fairness and discernment.
Help us to hear your voice in the midst of our discussions,
and to respond with alacrity to your call,
however challenging it may be, or whatever sacrifice it may require.
Like Solomon of old, give to us discerning hearts that we may lead your people well.
For Christ's sake.
Amen

Journeying with Joseph

Janet Lunt

The big picture

Genesis, chapters 37 and 39—50

Begin by stilling yourself for several minutes, then read the story of Joseph, asking the Lord to open your mind and heart to hear it as if for the first time. You may want to jot down anything that stands out for you.

This is the story of Joseph, son of Jacob, who from an early age is a prophetic dreamer and man of God. He is favoured by his father, hated by his brothers, taken as a slave to Egypt and wrongly imprisoned there. Later, he is exonerated by the pharaoh himself through the use of his God-given gifts, and is eventually reconciled with his family.

As we look at various aspects of Joseph's life events, we will glean insights from his walk with God, and draw on symbolism that occurs in the story to aid our reflection and prayer.

Special coat

Genesis 37:1–4

Jacob gave to Joseph a coat that stirred up hatred in his brothers but that was also a powerful symbol. The Hebrew words for this special garment have been translated in many ways, including a long robe with sleeves, an elaborately embroidered coat, a decorated tunic and a richly ornamented robe. The only other identical Hebrew reference in the Old Testament is found in 2 Samuel 13:18, which refers to the garment of a princess. The robe has been made famous through the Rice/Lloyd-Webber musical as a coat of many colours, but regardless of whether it was multi-coloured, embroidered or stylish, it spoke of specialness. It was a gift from a father, blatantly showing favouritism to his young son. Yet, from our vantage point, it seems to be a fitting symbol of a multifaceted and later adaptable character, steadfast in faith, gifted and favoured by God. As the story unfolds, we watch Joseph become a resourceful and capable person, and a truly great and godly leader. Perhaps Jacob knew Joseph well and loved what he saw: a lively and intelligent character, a son with a strong and upright faith who would uphold the ways of Yahweh into the next generation, and someone who met with God in dreams, not unlike himself. Although the special coat was destroyed, what it symbolised could not be.

If your heavenly Father made a coat especially for you, what might it look like and represent? What would be the features, colours, decoration? Spend some time reflecting on, and giving thanks for, your strengths, personality and gifts, God-given and nurtured.

Draw your own symbolic coat by creating a simple outline that fills most of an A4 sheet, then draw and colour items within it that symbolise who you are. Alternatively, you could decorate it with a collage of words. There will be opportunities to add to your coat over the next two weeks.

The shadow side

Genesis 37:3–35

Joseph's relationship with some of his older half-brothers was put under strain by the open favouritism their father showed him. 'Telling tales' of their bad behaviour, encouraged by Jacob, did not help. No wonder the gift of the famous coat caused such resentment. The final straw came when Joseph shared his dreams. Was it an adolescent lack of discernment to share them?

Jacob was extremely careless; he made it obvious that Rachel was his favourite wife, and her two sons his favourite children. Joseph, a 'goody-two-shoes' to his brothers, was naive, yet also an obedient son and serious about his faith. Was there more to this sibling rivalry than the way Jacob handled his family? Maybe the brothers resented Joseph's personality, giftedness and relationship with God, attributes that later impressed Potiphar, the jailer and Pharaoh. Perhaps his goodness, in sharp contrast to the past lives of his brothers, cast a shadow. The coat symbolised something that sickened his siblings, who took it from him at the well. They hoped to be rid of all it stood for.

It can be hard to come to terms with the favour God appears to bestow on some. Handling jealousy in a family is tricky, and differing ages, personalities, gifts and needs make it impossible to show equal treatment to each child. Yet to grow in wholeness, each needs to know they are loved and unique, alongside learning to celebrate others. We observe a similar conflict in the story of the prodigal son (Luke 15:11–32).

Hold a coin in your palm, 'tails' side up. Ponder the gifts and blessings in Joseph's life, and their shadow side, the imperfect reactions to them. Recall situations with family, church or colleagues where gifts or blessings have caused or are causing rivalry, favouritism or jealousy. Be honest about your own feelings and reactions. (Gifts might include success, looks, personality, popularity.) Talk with your heavenly Father about it all, seeking insight and wisdom.

When you're ready, turn the coin over to the 'heads' side; let it represent God's rule. Joseph trusted himself to God throughout his life. Offer in prayer your areas of struggle to God's rule, for his good outcomes and purposes.

In a foreign land

Genesis 37:25–28; 39:1

At some point in our lives, most of us experience unsettling, even disturbing times when we have to move to a new area or home, or change jobs, and feel as if we are in a foreign land with an unknown future. For the teenage Joseph it was particularly hard; his own flesh and blood had sold him to become a slave in another country and culture. He lost his family, status, familiar home setting and contact with the people of God. He would have to learn the language and customs of Egypt, and although the scriptures tell us that God was with him, he surely had moments of despair. He was imprisoned for many years through the lies of Potiphar's wife, for he was 30 when he was eventually released. There were no scriptures from which to take comfort in prison—they hadn't been written. Yet, as Joseph lived through servitude and many of his best years in false incarceration, he grew in wisdom and insight, and his trust remained firm in the God of Israel.

We can find ourselves in situations that imprison or trap us, that may make us feel alone in our faith. Although life can be tough, we are more fortunate than Joseph in that we have access to a wealth of scriptures and books to help us. Reading between the lines of this astonishing story, there is solace to be found, for we know the outcome is better than good. For us, there are vivid Bible images to hold on to, especially in the New Testament. Jesus, who described himself as shepherd, friend, vine and more, spoke many times of the kingdom of heaven, a kingdom we carry within us, and we are fed with metaphors such as our citizenship being in heaven (Philippians 3:20).

Think of a time when you felt that no one understood your situation. Read Psalm 137, reflecting on the heartache of a people imprisoned in a foreign land.

Compose your own psalm or lament, either expressing alienation you have experienced or empathy for people currently living in forced exile. End it with something that has helped you in the past or with an encouraging promise from scripture.

Transparency

Genesis 39:2–22

Heaven knows what terror and hardships accompanied Joseph on his journey from dry well to Egyptian slave market. Yet once there, he made the right choices about how to conduct himself. Potiphar was quick to recognise his qualities and soon trusted him completely with running his household. Joseph's faith remained intact and was not hidden from his master, who acknowledged that the God of the Hebrews was behind Joseph's success. Grateful for his meteoric rise from slavery, Joseph had a strong sense of loyalty both to God and to his human master, and showed great self-control in refusing the many advances of his master's wife. But for all his goodness, he fell at the hands of this scorned woman. His qualities now stood in her way.

Today, adverts flaunt brands and designer labels to demonstrate power and success. The popularity of some brands has plagued parents as their offspring demand expensive labels to keep up with their peers. Society places huge importance on outward appearance, image, status and youthful looks. But God looks on the inside. In the book *Mister God, This Is Anna*, by Fynn (Fount, 1987, p. 13) the six-year-old Anna declares that the difference between a person and an angel is easy: 'Most of an angel is in the inside and most of a person is on the outside.'

Joseph could perhaps be described as transparent, a man of integrity. He had risen from loin cloth to respectable tunic but, once again, his garment was taken from him, this time to be used as false evidence against him. Yet, naked or dressed, in loin cloth or robes, he remained pleasing in God's eyes. He always wore the God label. How would we stand up in such a situation?

Read Colossians 3:12–17. The version from THE MESSAGE provides a helpful opening image: 'So, chosen by God for this new life of love, dress in the wardrobe God picked out for you: compassion, kindness, humility, quiet strength, discipline…'

Which items of 'inner clothing' do you recognise in Joseph? Ask the Holy Spirit to make you aware of any part of your inner wardrobe you may have discarded that God chose for you to wear. Make it your designer label this week. Write it on a clothes label and safety-pin it inside one of your garments or perhaps into the neck of your coat, so that you will be reminded of it frequently. Alternatively, use a sticky-backed label.

In God's time

Genesis 39:21—40:22

A repeated line in this epic story is, 'The Lord was with Joseph and gave him success in whatever he did' (see 39:3, 23). The word 'success' is probably not one we would apply today to such a lengthy and unfair time in jail. We have no idea whether he protested his innocence or had moments of despair, but we can assume that he made the best of the time, behaving responsibly, for soon the jailer trusted him. We witness here an innocent young man, hugely wronged twice, who nevertheless stood by his God. Joseph's success was that the Lord was with him. Whatever his feelings from day to month to year, we learn that Joseph was ready to serve with his God-given gift. His employment in looking after the king's servants in prison revealed God at work, for Joseph was in the right place at the right time to hear and interpret their dreams.

In our 'instant' society of smart phones and tablet computers, it is hard to wait for things that are not immediate. Important issues, such as global warming, are soon swallowed up in the latest demands of a busy, success-driven lifestyle. Conversely, in the kingdom of heaven we find that experience and waiting with openness are essential to attune to God's 'voice' and to gain wisdom to weigh potential revelation.

The outcome of Joseph's story is already known to us: an unparalleled future. Therefore, with hindsight, we can see God's timing. However, waiting is a tough pastime for the best of people, especially when circumstances are unfair and God seems silent or inactive. Like Joseph, we are not exempt from waiting, but God's intentions are always to give 'a hope and a future' (Jeremiah 29:11, NIV). In God's time, Joseph was raised to a position of respect within the jail, and later restored and promoted to the highest rank in the land under Pharaoh. His progress is a reminder that Jesus said we would have trouble in this world (John 16:33), but that he would send the Holy Spirit to help us. This is crowned with a promised share in his glory.

Joseph might have worded Genesis 39:23 as follows: 'The Lord is with me and gives me success in all I do.' Try saying this out loud in relation to your own journey. How does it make you feel?

The following scripture promises relate to time and waiting: Psalm 27:13–14; Jeremiah 29:11; Isaiah 40:31. Allow them to speak to you.

Bring to mind any struggles you have with timing or waiting. Bring them in honesty to the Lord. Complete the following sentence, 'In God's time…' Prayerfully write your sentence, and any of the above, on your 'special coat', perhaps along the hemline or weaving it around something relevant you have already drawn.

Forgotten

Genesis 40:12–15, 20–23

Alas! Joseph was completely forgotten by Pharaoh's steward. He remained in the dungeon, despite the cup-bearer's experiencing godly revelation through him, witnessing the cook's fate and being spared himself. Perhaps the restored steward forgot Joseph because he was still afraid of Pharaoh's earlier anger and was busy proving his worth.

There are times when being forgotten can smart, especially after making an effort for someone. It can on occasion be devastating, and in some circumstances a grateful response can mean the difference between a satisfactory and a ruined relationship. Conversely, it is easy and occasionally convenient to forget others when we are busy or things are going well. Forgetfulness and ingratitude were on Jesus' mind after he healed ten lepers of illness, freeing them from stigma, and only one returned to thank God on being declared clean (Luke 17:11–19).

Joseph, of course, had to rely solely on his own experience of faith to see him through the hard knocks of injustice, being forgotten and having no freedom. We are not given details of how he maintained his hope and courage, but we can find comfort from many illuminating words in the Bible. Isaiah provides a particularly powerful example in Isaiah 49:15–16.

In our society, there are so many freedoms to be grateful for, yet much is taken for granted, and it is often only when confronted with the great needs of others, or when we lose something, that we truly appreciate what we have. Taking stock every now and then of all we have is a good exercise in gratitude.

Imagine being in Joseph's company at the point when all hope of being remembered fades. Envisage him at prayer in his dark and damp cell. How does he pray?

If you can, go for a walk today, being mindful of your many freedoms, and thanking God for them. Or use your freedom of choice in another way; you could buy a concert ticket or phone a friend.

A new robe, a new beginning

Genesis 41:1–45

At last, Joseph is remembered and summoned. His gift is needed. He shaves and puts on clean clothes—rituals important to the Egyptians, which could be viewed as symbolic of the moment from which he will never look back. His interpretation of the dream and sound advice on how to proceed in the face of disaster bring relief to the king. Pharaoh welcomes God at work through Joseph, granting him the top job in the land. It is an extraordinary new beginning, beyond Joseph's wildest dreams. This defining moment is appropriately marked by the giving of new robes of nobility, the pharaoh's own ring, and a new name meaning, 'God lives and speaks'.

Looking back, Jacob's gift of the special coat appears to have been a prophetic symbol, but this time his son has a special robe that won't be taken from him. Joseph's God-gift, which caused rejection by his family, has now brought him restoration in Egypt, and his integrity commands respect and authority. The new appointment will utilise Joseph's talents fully. Some parallels can be drawn here between the stories of Joseph and Nelson Mandela. Also, we are reminded again of the prodigal son, who received a new robe and ring on being restored, and both stories end with family celebrations as all are united in love.

People often mark a significant milestone in their lives. Sometimes they receive a new name or title, such as at baptism and other rites of passage, or when a person commits to a religious order. Think of any defining moments on your spiritual journey and how they were marked.

Find a white pebble or another attractive stone. Read Revelation 2:17, from the letter to the church in Pergamum. It is thought that the white stone or pebble could be a symbol of an entry ticket to the heavenly banquet. Reflect on this, using the pebble in your hand to aid your imagination. What might be written on it?

Create a new name or phrase for God that expresses what you love, praise and honour about him—for example, Immortal Light, Protecting Father, Hope-giving Friend. Use it to address God in prayer.

In scarcity and in plenty

Genesis 41:46–57

'Can we find anyone like this man, one in whom is the spirit of God?' declared Pharaoh (v. 38), as he entrusted the future of the nation to our hero. The predicted years of plenty were very good. Joseph married and had two children, naming them after his blessings. In his new role, he kept true to God's word, supervising the storage of all the extra grain, so much that it was beyond measuring. What a wonderful image of God's generous provision.

During the years of famine, news travelled abroad of grain to spare in Egypt. Joseph was well prepared and therefore able to handle the influx of hungry people. In contrast to his careful preparation during a time of plenty, we could reflect on our nation's squandering of North Sea oil as if it would last forever. We are all aware, as well, that the earth produces more than enough to meet everyone's needs, but greed, possessiveness and politics prevent the resources from being distributed evenly. Many starve despite food mountains, and there are some governments who won't allow food aid to reach their own hungry people.

The famous verses in Ecclesiastes 3 speak eloquently of contrasting seasons in life: a time to give and another to receive, times of joy and of loss; and Paul, who experienced times of both need and plenty, spoke about learning the secret of being content in any situation, saying that he could do all this through the One who gave him strength (Philippians 4:12–13).

Find a favourite piece of quiet music, one that helps you to be at ease in the presence of God, and have it ready to play. Find a comfortable position and still your thoughts. Check that your body is relaxed; become aware of sounds, your own breathing; then in this space, slowly let go of all distractions, things that cling, all ambition, all impatience, your anxieties.

Turn your thoughts to our living planet, and marvel at all of nature silently growing; imagine all that is going on right now worldwide— babies being born, people dying, folk at work, at leisure, asleep, building, chatting, crying, gambling, plotting, innovating; think of your place in this teeming world with all its love and creativity, all its problems and conflict.

Now, play the music; ask the Lord for inner contentment and calm for whatever this day, week and even year might bring, and rest in God's presence.

Mixed emotions

Genesis 42:1—45:15

The last thing Joseph ever expected was to see members of his family again, and he had to deal with it on the spot. Here, perhaps for the first time, we see Joseph's human side. Despite his position of strength, both as governor and as the unrecognised party, the presence of his brothers put him on the defensive. Suddenly he wasn't transparent— he spoke harshly and played games with them. We don't know if his overriding motive was to wield power, to give them a taste of their own medicine, or simply to see Benjamin and his father again, but Joseph made them sweat. All the same, he was often overwhelmed with emotion. What bitter-sweet sorrow to hear his brothers expressing, in his native Hebrew, fear of God and regret for what they had done to him in his youth!

The tables had turned. The brothers discovered what it was like to fear the unknown and to be at the mercy of an apparent stranger. Joseph didn't provide 'instant-fix' reconciliation, for he had no way of knowing if they were better men. He tested them. Slowly, he discovered that they were being honest, felt remorse and cared deeply for Jacob and Benjamin. Whatever turmoil he suffered, love for his family proved stronger, and finally Joseph revealed his identity. Reconciliation followed.

Think about times when forgiveness has been straightforward and other times when it has been a longer, painful process. We cannot circumnavigate Jesus' teaching on the subject, but forgiveness needs to be real, and that can take time.

The creation of a pearl provides a helpful analogy for the transformation forgiveness can bring. The process begins when a foreign substance enters an oyster or mussel shell. To protect itself, the creature surrounds the irritant with layers of iridescent secretion normally used to create the shell's lining. Jean-Paul Richter (German writer, 1763–1825) wrote: 'The heart that forgives an injury is like the perforated shell of a mussel which closes its wound with a pearl' (quoted in Giles and Meville Harcourt, *Short Prayers for a Long Day*, Liguori Publishing, 1996, p. 163).

Find a ball of wool and something small and rough, such as a piece of rock, fragment of splintered wood, short prickly stem, or teasel. Begin to cover the item by winding wool around it. It may be difficult to hide the 'irritant' and could take some time (you might need to continue later). As it is transformed, let the action speak. Ponder God's extraordinary forgiveness, and your own ability to forgive through his enabling.

Blessing

Genesis 45:16—49:28

God's generosity during the good harvests was likened to the grains of sand on the seashore. Pharaoh and his court were blessed to experience God's care for their people through prophetic and practical means. The Egyptians valued Joseph so highly that his newly-discovered family were treated with undeserved kindness by the pharaoh himself. From now on, Joseph's kin would be blessed by being near him, as others had been (see Genesis 39:5). Joseph saved his brothers from hunger, from themselves and from their past. He was able to be with his father again and at his bedside when he died. These chapters are filled with blessings for Jacob, for his children and grandchildren. What was broken had been restored by God through Joseph.

Jesus came to humanity to bring life in its fullness, to bless us with fulfilment of heart and soul. His life and death formed an act of the greatest possible generosity. We are taught that it is more of a blessing to give than to receive, and we hear more about generosity and blessing, giving and receiving in 2 Corinthians 9:6, 8: 'Whoever sows generously will also reap generously... And God is able to bless you abundantly, so that in all things at all times, having all that you need, you will abound in every good work.' These verses describe the rhythm or cycle of love that will bring God's kingdom on earth.

The presence of God with Joseph had a radiating effect, blessing those around him. We are also called to this, called to be the aroma or fragrance of Christ in the world (2 Corinthians 2:15).

Reflect on the thought that you carry with you the presence of the One who blesses in abundance. Let this inspire you for a time of intercession for people and situations on your heart. You could begin and end your prayers with the following verses from Ephesians 3:20–21: 'Now to him who is able to do immeasurably more than all we ask or imagine, according to his power that is at work within us, to him be glory in the church and in Christ Jesus throughout all generations, forever and ever! Amen.'

Plan to do something extravagantly generous this week.

Vision and dreaming

Genesis 49:29—50:26

Reunited with his family, Joseph now saw the full picture of God's vision for his life. He had been sent ahead by God to Egypt to be made Pharaoh's chief counsellor in order to save many lives, and to ensure the future of Abraham's descendants. When the brothers sought fresh assurance of forgiveness after Jacob's death, Joseph could say with no regret that God had made it turn out for the best. Just before his own death, he re-envisioned his family with God's plan to lead them to the land promised to their forefathers. He asked one thing of them, to take his remains with them to be buried there. Later, under Moses, the people of Israel carried Joseph's bones on their epic journey through the wilderness (Exodus 13:19). In her book *Lighted Windows* (BRF, 2002), Margaret Silf speaks of them carrying 'the symbol of their God-dream', and of our dream being the energy that sustains us on our journey.

Joseph was a dreamer and prophet, and a faithful servant of the society that restored him. His confidence lay with God. Throughout his life he never shrank from speaking of the One who reveals himself to humanity; he shared what he received from God, without knowing if the recipients would respond or not; he was bold, clear and sometimes blunt. Our culture is very different, and our experiences are rarely as dramatic as those of Joseph, but his openness to receive and share God's dream challenges us.

Dreams help us to focus, giving us hope and direction, and lie behind the journey to much achievement. God dreamed and the universe came into being. We are part of that dream, and God has given us gifts, hearts and minds to fulfil our part in it. When we dream with God, we have something wonderful to share.

How would you describe God's dream for humanity? What are your dreams?

Design a poster or create a card expressing your thoughts. Use artwork or calligraphy, or simply write appropriate words in a ready-made picture card. Be open to displaying it in your home, or giving it to someone who needs to dream again.

Return to your own 'special coat' and write your dreams into it. Take a look at all you have learnt from Joseph's journey.

Lent: wilderness time

Bridget Hewitt

Into the wilderness

> *Then Jesus was led up by the Spirit into the wilderness to be tempted by the devil. He fasted forty days and forty nights, and afterwards he was famished.*
>
> MATTHEW 4:1–2, NRSV

So begins the Gospel for the first Sunday of Lent. This story, the story of the temptations in the wilderness, has given us the format, the 40 days, for Lent. It is the story of the beginning of Jesus' ministry. After his baptism and the great affirmation that came to him at that point, he was 'led by the Spirit', compelled in some way to spend time alone, to be thrust off any pedestal that the affirming moment of his baptism might have put him on, and to find out who he really was, what form his ministry was to take.

It is a moment in the Church's year for us too to take stock, to let ourselves be asked questions as to who we really are, to delve beneath some of the baggage that makes up the normal agenda of our life.

So, as we come to the beginning of Lent, let's ask ourselves how and in what way the Spirit may be trying to lead us 'into the wilderness', into some space or place or time where we may hear a voice that comes from a deeper place than that of the chaotic confusion that can surround so much of our lives, where we may hear the questions that hold our true selves in the balance, that offer us the road to life.

Where and how do I find wilderness space? For each of us it will be different, because each of our lives and circumstances are different, but the question and the challenge is there for all of us. In our fast-moving world it is never going to be easy to give ourselves permission to stop, to enter 'wilderness'. It may feel wrong. It may feel a waste of time. It may feel like an indulgence. Such voices are loud and clear in our heads. But the Spirit, quietly, persistently, is giving us this opportunity. 'The gate is narrow… that leads to life' (Matthew 7:14).

The time that we can each give to this wilderness space will vary, but the discipline of putting aside time may be the most important thing we do during these coming weeks. The extent of the time and what we do with it will be different for everyone: for some it may be daily, for others once a week. What matters is to make the attempt.

Some 'wilderness' ideas: half an hour, perhaps reading a book that may feed you on the spiritual journey; a walk or cycle ride in the countryside; time spent sitting and playing with your children rather than rushing to the next activity; time set aside once a day, once every other day, once a week, for drawing, painting, writing poetry; time spent in an empty church, quietly, on your own; regular meditation time. These are just a few ideas—everyone will have their own.

Give yourself permission! Jesus was 'led by the Spirit into the wilderness'. You too, perhaps, are being led: *listen* to that inner voice, often shrouded by the clouds of over-busyness.

A prayer to ponder

Spend some time with this prayer today, as you begin the Lenten journey. Go slowly through the phrases, allowing each part to speak in your heart. Try not to rush in with thoughts and answers, but rather to let the thoughts that it evokes speak gently in your depths.

Creating God
You are mothering me into life:
As I stand at this threshold in the Church's year, you are calling me into greater freedom, greater wholeness; to cleansing and inner growth.
How might I use these days?
How might you be calling me?
What sort of wilderness are you nudging me towards?
What sort of inner stripping do I need, in order to grow towards greater wholeness?

Help me to set aside time, to pause and use this opportunity offered by the weeks of Lent.
Help me to listen to the small voice in my own depths, beckoning me, or perhaps buffeting me, towards wilderness, towards space, towards 'being'.
I want to resist.
'I don't have time. It isn't that important. It's irresponsible. I have too much else to do.'
So many voices tell me not to take time out.

Yet you, God, are calling me to step off the rollercoaster that runs my life.
Help me, oh Lord, to listen, to hear, to respond.
Give me the courage to take the time,
So that I may begin to hear that whisper of a different voice in the depths of my own heart.
Help me,
Help me,
To respond.
Amen

Unwanted wilderness time

Wilderness time, unwanted and unasked for, may be thrust upon us. The onset of sudden illness, the death of a loved one, loss in all its variety of ways—these are some of the wilderness situations that life throws at us, that can make us suddenly and acutely aware of our human frailty. At such times we may cry out in desperation to a God who seems far away, only to have our cries echoed back at us down a wasteland of emptiness. In these wilderness situations we long for a God who, as Jesus was tempted to do, could indeed turn our stones into bread.

Many of us, we hope, are not living in such a time, but we all hover on that threshold. And here, in these early days of Lent, it is worth pausing on the threshold and simply asking ourselves to stand there. Stand at the doorway of the immense suffering that so many in this world are experiencing. Suffering, confusion, senselessness. There are many, many such doorways, staring into that desert land of meaninglessness.

There are no facile answers to these agonising wildernesses of our lives.

We long for stones to be turned into bread.

We yearn and cry out for a perfect world where suffering is no longer…

But it is not to be.

For today, stand there. Stand and 'feel' the pain and the meaninglessness, and breathe into the present moment of reality—a reality which, for so many, is one of anguish, abandonment, horror, and in which, perhaps, God simply 'is not'. And yet we hold on to another reality, that God, the God who is love, utterly vulnerable, is there, hanging on that cross of eternal powerlessness. The pain will not go, but love—and mystery—remain. For today, stand at the foot of that cross, and, with Christ, feel the pain.

Listening to God

> 'If you are the Son of God, command these stones to become
> loaves of bread.'
> MATTHEW 4:3

We so much want everything to be all right! We want to be able to
control our lives. But there are always aspects of life that we cannot
control.

> 'One does not live by bread alone, but by every word that
> comes from the mouth of God.'
> MARK 4:4

How do we *hear* or *understand* words that come from the mouth of God?

In the Gospel story it was Jesus' hunger that initiated both this
temptation and his response to it.

It may be that we too need to be emptied in some way before we can
begin to hear a deeper wisdom, hear that song underneath, the voice
of God that is so often hidden.

In the story of the rich young man (Mark 10:17–22), Jesus, looking
at him with love, told him that he lacked one thing. Read slowly
through that story. Imagine Jesus looking at you with *love*. Rest for a
few moments with that phrase.

That love sees through all the 'parts' of you,
The parts you don't like or feel ashamed of,
The parts and episodes that you want to forget,
The worries and anxieties and fears,
The jobs you do, the roles you play.

Imagine Jesus gazing at you, knowing you, loving you in all your
littleness: just loving you as *you*. 'You lack one thing,' he says. 'Go,

69

sell what you own and give…'

In the story Jesus knew that it was his riches that were preventing the young man from truly following the way of God.

For each of us those 'riches' will be different, but they will always be things, thoughts, attitudes, memories that we *cling* to, that are preventing us moving out into greater freedom, into a space where we may hear the words of God in our hearts.

'You lack one thing… Go, sell…' Let Jesus speak these words to *you*. Let him speak in the deep places of your being.

What do I need to give up, or to let go, in order to hear, just that little bit more clearly, the voice of God, the voice of life?

Noticing beauty

Beauty is something that may help us to hear the voice of God. Find time today to notice beauty. So often we rush along and fail really to see what is right in front of us. So today, stop! And look!

Go into a garden or green space.

Notice the bulbs and flowers and blossom,

The leaves uncurling on the trees,

The birdsong…

And pause as you see and listen.

Pause, wonder,

Let a smile arise in your heart.

Notice other people, look at faces as you pass them in the street, in the office, in the doctor's surgery, wherever you are—the wonderful varied rainbow of God's people:

> *Christ plays in ten thousand places,*
> *Lovely in limbs, and lovely in eyes not his*
> *To the Father through the features of men's faces.*
> GERARD MANLEY HOPKINS, *POEMS AND PROSE*, PENGUIN CLASSICS, 1974, P. 51

Beauty manifests itself in so many forms. It is a gift, God's voice speaking in tones we so often do not stop to hear. God does not force himself upon us, but the offering is all around us. As Jacob came to recognise, 'The Lord is in this place—and I did not know it! … This is the gate of heaven!' (Genesis 28:16–17). The gate of heaven is indeed everywhere. So let your inner eyes open—and see!

Faces of pride

In the second temptation (Matthew 4:5–7), Jesus is tempted to throw himself off the highest pinnacle of the temple, to prove that God will keep him safe.

What is Jesus being asked to prove in this temptation? Or, more personally, what are *we* being asked to become aware of in ourselves?

It is a cunning temptation, couched in the language of proving that God will look after me. How easy it is for us to think we are doing God's will while in fact we are strengthening our own identities, our own worlds of desire, our longing for success and achievement! How we fall into this trap of ego-enhancement, again and again!

Jesus' response, 'Do not put the Lord your God to the test' (v. 7), is a response of vulnerability. Whatever lies ahead of him, whatever his life's work or mission will be, it is not going to be about God's bolstering up his pride in his *abilities* so that these abilities give him his identity. And so it is with us. We all have abilities, of course, and they are important. But there is a subtle difference between knowing our strengths and abilities, and assuming our identity through them. This temptation alerts us to the dangers of pride and the response of humility. It is in our 'nothingness' that God comes to us, and from there our abilities can be put to use—but only from that place, not the other way round.

As you pray today, let your mind run over the past week and your plans for the coming week, and simply allow yourself to become aware of how much 'pride', in one way or another, is tied up with so many of your thoughts and actions.

Don't judge yourself; just become aware. Such motivations are part of all of us, and to an extent are necessary, of course: we have to make plans, and things need to be done. The danger is in feeling that your worth is in your achievements.

So in prayer today just become aware: aware of your plans and hopes, aware of some of your motives, your achievements, and aware of how little and vulnerable you really are underneath all of these things.

If you can, sit with this for a while, letting God's love for your vulnerable human self surround you.

Free to be you

Opening ourselves to self-awareness and self-knowledge is not always comfortable or easy, and some of those thoughts from the previous session may have been disquieting.

God, however, is always love. And love always calls us to life.

An exercise with stones

Find a stone and hold it, feeling its weight. Let it symbolise all that weighs you down, all sadness, guilt, anxiety; all anger, distress. *Feel* whatever is weighing you down. Stay with this for a while, really feeling the weight in that stone. Sometimes it may be helpful to put several stones in a bag and feel the weight of that. Make sure that, in your imagination, you are putting in all that weighs you down: *all* of it. Hold it, or try to hold it, for long enough really to feel the weight.

Now drop your stones: simply drop them. Open your hands and let them go. Feel the loss of that weight. This relief, this lightness and joy, is what God is calling you to.

Light as a feather
Vulnerable as a feather
Beautiful as a feather
This is God's calling to you.
This is who you really are!

So go—and be...!

Into the void

Today we ponder another side to this temptation: the times when pride may prevent us throwing ourselves off the pinnacle. Are there times when we hold on to security or self-esteem too tightly?

Maybe we are frightened of making a fool of ourselves.

Maybe we are frightened of confrontation or of someone else's pain.

These are times when we need to lose our firm footing, to throw ourselves out of our safety nets, out of familiar modes of being. For while it is pride that tells us to jump off the pinnacle in order to show our own worth, it is equally pride that prevents us from taking the leap into the dark for fear of dinting our self-esteem. Jesus could, presumably, have remained safely well away from the wilderness, after the great affirming moment of his baptism, but he did not.

The 'devil' of the Bible is cunning indeed, because he—or she—is so often right. The difference between the way of the devil and the way of Jesus is that one offers a way to build a false ego-self, while the other the way to transcend ego and let go into ever-expanding life. And once we throw ourselves into *that* void, painful or difficult as it may be, the arms of the Divine are indeed around us.

The question is how to tell the difference, how to discern the wiles and guises of pride.

Spend some time with these thoughts, asking yourself in what areas of your life pride may perhaps be preventing you from taking that plunge into the unknown, from jumping off your safe ground.

What sort of pedestals have I created for myself, on which I feel safe and secure?

Read the story of Peter walking on water (Matthew 14:28–33).

What 'boat' might you be stuck in, in your life, right now?

What might be preventing you from taking that radical leap of madness/faith?

A meditative walk

This question of pride, wrapping itself cunningly around us, is dealt with by Jesus in his response to the tempter: 'Do not put the Lord your God to the test.'

Try to take some time, perhaps going for a walk on your own, quietly repeating this phrase to yourself. Let it gradually unfold within you.

Ponder on it, letting it speak to your heart.

How do we trust a God who is not to be put to the test?

How do we trust a God who may often seem to be absent?

How do we trust a God who allows himself to be killed?

These questions come to us as we follow the way of Jesus into all the emptiness of the cross, and there are no easy answers.

Yet we are called, as was Jesus, to allow space within our own depths for this extraordinary God to fan into flame that spark of divine love that is the true calling of humanity.

Do not put the Lord your God to the test, no, but allow space for God to arise.

'The kingdom of God is not coming with things that can be observed… the kingdom of God is among you' (Luke 17:20–21).

Trust in the living God who dwells within and amongst us, in the utmost vulnerability of love.

Living in the ocean of God's love

'All these [kingdoms of the world] I will give you, if you fall down and worship me.'
MATTHEW 4:9

Our egos do not sit still.

Even after the prayer of yesterday, we may find ourselves yearning again for 'the kingdoms of the world and their splendour' (v. 8). If I could get this particular bit of my life out of the way, then... If I could buy that house, that car, redecorate my room in this way, then... If I could find the perfect partner in life, then... If, in whatever way, I could just make this or that particular bit of my life more perfect, then everything would be so much better. We will all recognise these feelings in one way or another.

But Jesus has had enough. 'Away with you, Satan!' he says. Stop this nagging dissatisfaction with what is; this feeling that the grass is always greener somewhere other than where I am now. Find out what it means to 'worship the Lord your God and serve only him' (v. 10).

The medieval English mystic, Julian of Norwich, was shown in one of her visions something as small as a hazelnut in the palm of her hand. She came to realise, through this vision, that this *littleness* was the reality of everything, and the reason everything existed at all was because God loved it.

> He showed me a little thing, the size of a hazelnut, on the palm of my hand... I looked at it thoughtfully and wondered, 'What is this?' The answer came, 'It is all that is made... It exists, both now and forever, because God loves it.' In short, everything owes its existence to the love of God.
>
> JULIAN OF NORWICH, *REVELATIONS OF DIVINE LOVE*, PENGUIN CLASSICS, 1998, P. 68

A suggestion for meditation today: take something small: a leaf, a pebble, a shell. Hold it in the palms of your hands as you ponder on Julian's vision.

Feel the littleness, the fragility…

Hold it for a while, letting your heart wonder…

Let those words sing in your heart: 'this is all that is made… it exists… because God loves it.'

This God who does not turn stones into bread, who does not value us according to our abilities, who is not interested in the powers of the world, is known by *love*, and *is* love, and invites us to enter into that love, and to learn how to love. We are surrounded by an infinite ocean of love; we need simply to become aware of it and to let it gently break over us.

Living in the present moment

Today we think again about Jesus' response: 'Worship the Lord your God and serve only him' (Matthew 4:10).

What might this mean?

How do we truly worship and serve God?

'I am who I am,' God told Moses (Exodus 3:14). Not 'I was' or 'I will be,' but I am.

God is here, right now, in this moment.

The more we can 'be' in the present moment, the more we will truly worship God rather than our own 'kingdoms' of plans, worries and meandering thoughts. God is eternally Now.

We spend much of our lives being somewhere other than where we are, and even when we try to stop for a while, our minds travel: back over past thoughts, forward into future plans, or ranging around the day's news and events.

Try to spend some time today in silent prayer.

Find a comfortable space where you will not be disturbed. Sit, preferably upright and supported, with both feet on the floor. Some may prefer to be cross-legged on the floor or on a prayer stool.

It may help if you are able to begin by listening to some music.

Gently become aware of your breathing, letting it slow down and lengthen.

As God breathed into creation to bring it to life, so God is breathing life into you with every breath you take.

Your thoughts will wander as you sit in this silent prayer.

Some find it helpful to have a word to hold on to, a word such as 'God', 'love', 'open', 'presence', 'Jesus', or you may have your own already.

Try to spend between ten and 20 minutes in silence, simply being present.

At the end you may feel that your mind has travelled miles while your body has been still. Don't worry. Don't judge yourself.

The great thing with this type of prayer is to return again and again to your word or your breath: each time you do this you are returning to the Now, to God, right here, right now.

Angels

Then the devil left him and suddenly angels came and waited on him.
MATTHEW 4:11

Angels come in various forms: words of comfort, a brief smile of love on the face of a suffering person; a sigh of shared pain; a sense of inner joy, a sudden shaft of sun across clouded skies, and many other ways, which we become aware of as we open our heart to their possibility.

The Bible presents us with the temptations Jesus faced in the wilderness, but they are in fact temptations of the human condition which, if we take the faith journey seriously, we face every day of our lives. They will not cease to assail us, but as long as we keep returning to that wilderness, acknowledging our littleness, confronting the games our egos want to play, and do not shy away from the discipline of inner awareness, we will without any doubt be given glimpses of angels, always there, waiting to serve us.

Have you met any angels along the way during these past two weeks? Bring them to mind, perhaps praying with these words:

He reached down from on high, he took me... He brought me into an open place, he rescued me because he delighted in me.
PSALM 18:16, 19

'Blessed be the name of God from age to age... He reveals deep and hidden things... and light dwells with him.'
DANIEL 2:20, 22

Let them speak inside your heart, and give thanks.

You may like to light a candle, placing it in front of you as a sign of thankfulness.

Lent: pausing on the way

Sally Smith

A place to rest

Several times we read of Jesus pausing at Bethany. Luke tells us that in the last week of his life Jesus spent each night on the Mount of Olives (21:37), another of Jesus' favourite places to escape to, and it was here that he spoke to his disciples of the coming of the Son of Man (Matthew 24). I like to think he might also have gone to spend some time that week with his friends Mary and Martha and Lazarus in nearby Bethany, retreating from the city to the quiet in the surrounding area and the safety of his friends' home.

It is fitting, therefore, that we pause here for a while partway through Lent, pausing on our way as Jesus did on his journey to Jerusalem and the cross. We will look at some of the events and characters associated with Bethany and spend some time simply resting with God.

After the raising of Lazarus, Jerusalem became a very dangerous place for Jesus. He knew that the authorities were trying to kill him. He knew he was going to die very soon, and he was trying to prepare his disciples for this. The escape to Bethany would have been significant to him at this time.

Where is your Bethany? Where do you escape to when it all becomes too much? Where do you go when you need to recharge your batteries ready for the next day? I have some favourite walks that do this. I am fortunate that my local church is open during the day and I creep in and spend time in the stillness with God, often at times when I have a lot to tell him and I'm struggling to hear his voice in the midst of everything else. I also have a bench in the garden where I often sit with a mug of coffee and have a quiet moment with God. Recognising your Bethany places can be useful in realising their importance and reminding you to revisit them more often. But be ready to find new Bethany places as well.

Geography of the area

The Mount of Olives is a range of four small summits just outside Jerusalem, separated by the deep Kidron Valley. It commands good views of Jerusalem and in Jesus' day would have given a fine view of the temple as well as the rest of the city. Then, it would have been heavily wooded with the olive trees from which it gets its name. It is the site, or assumed site, of many events in the Bible, including being the place where David went when he was escaping Absalom (2 Samuel 15:30), the anticipated place of the Messiah's coming (Zechariah 14:4), one of Jesus' places to escape to (John 8:1), where Jesus explained the end of the age to his disciples (Matthew 24), and was visited by the apostles after Jesus' resurrection (Acts 1:12).

At the base of the Mount of Olives is the garden of Gethsemane. The name Gethsemane comes from the oil press, where the oil would have been squeezed from the olives grown on the mount.

On the other side of the Mount of Olives is Bethany, home of Lazarus and his sisters, Mary and Martha. Bethany is on the main road from Jericho to Jerusalem, but out of sight of Jerusalem. It was a place that provided Jesus with the necessary place of rest and the space to prepare for the next day whenever he stayed there. It was the start of the Palm Sunday journey (Mark 11:1–11). As the home of Lazarus, Mary and Martha, it was the site of Jesus' meeting with them (Luke 10:38–42) and the raising of Lazarus (John 11:1–44) and his anointing in the house of Simon the leper (Mark 14:3–9). Bethany means 'house of the poor', which can be an interesting name to keep in mind when reading some of the stories of the village.

We will be looking at some of these events over the next two weeks, but you might like to look up the Bible references and begin to get a feel for these places. If you have access to the internet, you could look for photos of Bethany and the Mount of Olives and learn a bit more about them.

Mary anoints Jesus

Matthew (26:6–13) and Mark (14:3–9) place the anointing of Jesus at the home of Simon the leper in Bethany; John (12:1–8), however, places it in the home of Lazarus, and the woman who does the anointing is clearly identified as Mary. Here we use our imaginations to enter the scene, to begin to take part and draw closer to Jesus as we near Jerusalem and all that this place stands for. This is written for you to watch the scene; you may, however, prefer to enter more into the action—some might wish to become Mary and be the one who anoints Jesus' feet.

Imagine that you are in a room with Lazarus and Mary and several of the disciples. Spend some time looking around the room, noticing what is there, the size of the room. Watch the people—who do you recognise? Notice where you are in relation to the others: are you in the midst of all that is happening, or are you more on the edge, watching the occupants? Watch as Martha serves the food and drink. Begin to listen to some of the conversations. Sense the tension as Jesus' plans to go to Jerusalem are discussed. Do you join in any of the discussions, or just listen?

Notice Jesus in the room. Where is he sitting? Who is near him? Do you draw closer to him, or keep your distance?

Watch as Mary stands up and walks over to Jesus. She kneels at his feet and produces a small bottle. She carefully breaks off the top and pours the perfume over Jesus' feet. She wipes them with her hair. Smell the scent as it fills the house. What do you feel as she anoints Jesus' feet? Are you aware of the tension in the air from the disciples as they witness this shameless, extravagant act?

Watch Jesus as he enjoys the smell and the outpouring of perfume. Listen as someone says, 'Why was this perfume not sold for three hundred denarii and the money given to the poor?' Jesus responds, 'Leave her alone. She bought it so that she might keep it for the day of my burial. You always have the poor with you, but you do not always have me.'

Mary walks away from Jesus.

As the commotion dies down, Jesus calls you over to him. Do you go? How does that feel?

Sit with Jesus as he asks, 'What do you want from me?'

Respond from your heart and spend time with Jesus, in conversation or sitting quietly.

When you are ready, return to the room where you are sitting and recall some of the events that have taken place, particularly noting how you felt and your relationship and conversation with Jesus.

Anointing

We are familiar with the anointing of Jesus by Mary from the previous section, and with some of the women taking spices to anoint his body in the tomb after the sabbath, but how else was oil used in anointing in the Bible? In the Old Testament, it was used widely for anointing priests, and Exodus 29 describes in detail how this was to be done. It was also used in the consecration of the Ark of the Covenant and of the kings and prophets. Anointing was a sign of setting apart for God, of things and people being separated and dedicated to the service of

God. So the tabernacle and its furniture had a special function and were for the purpose of serving God.

When people were anointed, they were set apart for service to God, and in the New Testament this was generally accompanied by an outpouring of the Holy Spirit. So in 2 Corinthians 1:21–22 we read about Paul and Timothy being anointed by Christ and receiving the seal of ownership from Christ; in the anointing they were giving themselves and their work to Christ and allowing him to work with them. At that time Christ also 'put his Spirit in our hearts as a deposit, guaranteeing what is to come' (v. 22, NIV 1984).

As we pause partway through Lent, you might like to reflect on your journey with God, how you serve him, and your commitment to him in the future. As you do this, you might like to mark yourself with some oil to symbolise your gift of yourself to God and of receiving his gift and blessing on you. This could be a sign of the cross on your hands, committing the work of your hands (in whatever form that takes or may take) to God, or on your head as a sign of receiving his ownership of you and your receiving the Holy Spirit.

As you do this, receive God's good gifts to you.

You prepare a table before me in the presence of my enemies.
You anoint my head with oil; my cup overflows.
PSALM 23:5, NRSV

Martha's story

Luke 10:38–42

'Now that Jesus has gone and we've had some time to think about what happened when he was on earth and what he meant to us, I want to set the record straight. Some people have said things about me and what Jesus said to me that I don't think I agree with. I don't want people forever to think that I only did work in the kitchen and served, while my sister Mary did all the contemplation and listening to Jesus.

'It wasn't like that at all. I had heard that Jesus was coming to Bethany, and so I invited him to come and have a meal with us. It was a great honour for us to have him in our home. I wanted everything to be right, of course I did, and that was only fitting. If the neighbours got to hear that we hadn't offered the right hospitality, their tongues would never have stopped, but, more importantly, he was a good man and I wanted to do something for him. People were asking things from him, making demands on his energy and his time, and so I wanted to give him a break, let him rest and be looked after. It's something I can do—I believe I'm good at it. You could say that it's a God-given gift and that it would be wrong of me not to use it to serve others. It's also something I enjoy doing. Since that day, I have often welcomed people into our home and offered the same hospitality, and when I do that, it is like offering it to Jesus all over again. Sometimes, I know this sounds silly, but it is as if he is watching and thanking me for looking after his sheep.

'Sometimes Mary gets so involved in the mystical that she loses sight of the practical. I think she focuses too much on herself and her relationship with God and doesn't put what she learns into practice. She doesn't always live in the real world, and I thought that listening to Jesus might prompt some practical outworking of her immense love for God. It would be lovely to see her using some of her other gifts—I don't want to see them wasted. I don't think we have to be either in the kitchen or at the feet of Jesus; I think we can do both. In fact, I think the holiest people I know can do both and manage to balance them in their lives. I don't always get it right—well, not many of us do. Maybe I could spend more time listening to God and learning how much he loves me and showing my love for him directly, rather than through what I do.

'I was enjoying listening to what Jesus was saying as I worked in the kitchen. I missed a few bits, but Lazarus filled me in later, so that was okay. Without Jesus' teaching, I was just doing what I enjoyed and do well; and it was more about me and what I did. What Jesus made me realise was that it was about the people I'm serving: their needs are far more important than mine.

'Anyway, I just wanted to put the other side of the story. People might start thinking that I was criticising Mary, but I wasn't; neither was I moaning about having to do all the work—I enjoy it. Maybe we all sometimes need to look at the balance of action and contemplation. They complement each other, just like Mary and I do.'

You may want to consider how the Martha and Mary in you live together. Do they complement each other, or are they in conflict, each trying to assert their supremacy and vying for Jesus to praise them for what they do and who they are? Value the less dominant part of you and its contribution to making you into the person you are.

You might like to write your reply to Martha.

Mary's story

'I'm not like my sister Martha. She is brilliant at putting her faith into action. I prefer to sit and be with Jesus. I can sit for hours in prayer, gazing on a holy picture or a cross and just telling Jesus how much I love him. Martha thinks I'm wasting my time, but I don't think I am. As I grow closer to him I can serve him better in the things I do. People I meet say that they are fed with his peace when they spend time with me. It's different; they are fed with wonderful food cooked with love when they spend time with Martha. We all need both, and a few precious people manage to do both. Are you one of those?

'Why don't you try it now? Find a comfortable place. You may already have a favourite place to spend time with God. I do: it's on the Mount of Olives—a place where Jesus often went. I feel closer to him there.

'Then try just sitting and looking at a picture or the view around you. Wait and find God in what you see. Allow God to speak to you. He will. He may comfort you or challenge you. Hold on to what he says; it is so precious.

'I often think of the verse from Psalm 23 at these times: "He leads me beside quiet waters; he restores my soul" (Psalm 23:2–3, NIV 1984).

'At other times I imagine being back in our home in Bethany on that day, when I sat at his feet and listened. I tell him all the things that are bothering me, and listen as he reassures and instructs me all over again. It's the Holy Spirit working with my imagination, enabling me to hear the voice of God.'

Lazarus—Jesus delays

John 11:1–16

These events take place shortly before Jesus' own death and resurrection. When Jesus and his disciples hear that Lazarus is ill, Jesus does not immediately set off to Bethany. Instead, he waits for two days. He does not mention to his disciples that he has heard that Lazarus is ill. Neither does he send a message to Mary and Martha, who must have been waiting anxiously for his arrival, knowing that he could heal their brother and believing that he would want to heal his friend. Jesus does not appear to make any arrangement to go and visit Bethany in the near future.

To our eyes Jesus is delaying, and by his delay causing the death of Lazarus.

Eventually, Jesus arrives. Lazarus has been dead for four days. At the time it was believed that the spirit of a person left them after three days, so after four days there would be no question about the death of Lazarus.

In the delay, Jesus will have prayed for Lazarus and for his sisters. He will also have been praying about what was going to happen to him after Lazarus' resurrection. Raising someone from the dead was going to anger the already hostile authorities further, and the disciples are already anxious about Jesus' travelling to Judea. The raising of Lazarus determines the Jewish authorities in their plan to get rid of Jesus.

Jesus' delay ultimately brings glory to God. Jesus says that the illness will not lead to death but to God's glory, so that God's Son may be glorified through it (v. 4).

Pause and consider when you have delayed in taking action, and whether this has led to God's glory or taken the glory away. Are there any things you are delaying at the moment? How are you reducing or increasing God's glory through your inaction?

Are there things you should be praying for at the moment that you are avoiding?

Lazarus compared with Jesus

John 11:1–44

There are many connections and similarities between the death and resurrection of Lazarus and of Jesus. The death of Lazarus, coming so soon before the death of Jesus, in many ways points us towards the death of Jesus and prepares us for what is to happen. For example, in John 11:37 we read, 'Could not he who opened the eyes of the blind man have kept this man from dying?' compared with Matthew 27:42, 'He saved others... he can't save himself.' The question, 'Where have you laid him?' is asked on both occasions (see John 11:34 and 20:13–15).

In sharing the grief over the loss of his friend, Jesus is joining in the sorrow of humankind, as it says in Isaiah 53:4, 'Surely he has borne our griefs and carried our sorrows' (RSV). The Word made flesh weeps at the tomb of his friend and joins in the sorrow of the world.

Jesus doesn't come to Bethany all mighty and powerful, showing his divinity in a forceful act of power. Instead, he comes in tears, sharing and bearing the sorrow of his friends and of others around. Mary and Martha similarly bring their pain to Jesus with that 'if only'—if only you had come sooner, you could have saved him—which is rewarded by an explanation of resurrection. Jesus is explaining the future hope that he brings, not just now with Lazarus but in the times to come. He brings that future hope into present reality with the words, 'I am the resurrection and the life' (John 11:25).

At this point Jesus brings Lazarus to life, a mortal life from which Lazarus will eventually die, but pointing towards his own death and resurrection to a new eternal life.

You might like to read through the account of Lazarus' death and resurrection and see what resonances you encounter with the account of Jesus' own death and resurrection. How does this prepare you for the events to come in a few weeks? How could you represent these echoes visually?

Or you might prefer to join Mary and Martha in bringing your sorrow and pain to Jesus and allowing him to weep with you.

Lazarus—'come and see'

He said, 'Where have you laid him?' They said to him, 'Lord, come and see.'
JOHN 11:34, RSV

We have a similar comment at the beginning of John's Gospel when Andrew and another disciple asked Jesus where he was staying and

Jesus replied, 'Come and see' (1:46). Again, at the end of the Gospel, the risen Jesus invites the disciples, who have just made a miraculous catch of fish, to 'come and have breakfast' (21:12).

Jesus calls us to come and see, to lead us on from where we are. Mary and Martha invited him to 'come and see' where their pain and hurt was.

If you were able to invite Jesus to 'come and see', where would you lead him? It might be a place of pain, where you would like Jesus to be in the sorrow with you and to share the emotions and hurts. Or it might be a place of great joy from which you would like to praise him and offer your thanks for his graciousness and generosity.

Whichever is appropriate for you, invite Jesus to come with you to that place and share your feelings with him. Give him time to give to you, and take time to receive from him the good gifts he has to offer.

Then allow Jesus to say, 'Come and see' to you. Where does he lead you? What does he have to show you? What questions does this bring from you? Allow time with Jesus to ask these questions and to tell him about what you have seen.

Pausing

Psalms 42 and 43

These psalms are psalms of lament. They come from a place of pain and trouble and call out to a God who seems absent. Though they are numbered as two psalms, they are generally thought of as being one psalm in structure, sharing a refrain in verses 42:5, 42:11 and 43:5.

Settle down so that you are comfortable but alert. Recognise the thoughts you bring with you, and leave them in God's safekeeping as you pray.

Then turn to these two psalms. Read them through slowly a few times. It might help to read them aloud. Don't rush. If a word or phrase catches your attention, stay with it; if you stay there for the whole session, that's fine. Try to settle with one phrase that is calling you in some way.

Repeat this phrase in your head and allow your thoughts to work round it. When you have finished thinking, allow it to move from your head and into your heart, so that it becomes part of you. Receive it as being from God and allow him to speak to you through the phrase. Spend time with the phrase, without analysing it, but allowing it to speak to you in its own way.

When you are ready, you might like to respond to this phrase on paper. This could be in words, or you might take a pen or some crayons and represent something of your experience with the psalm. This should not be a direct representation, but an abstract interpretation of the essence of the psalm for you.

You might then like to reflect on this in your journal if you use one, considering how the psalm has changed for you.

Weeping over the city

Jesus set off from Bethany to Jerusalem, seated on a donkey. We usually focus on the triumphal entry with the crowds crying, 'Hosanna!' But in Luke 19:41–45 we read that Jesus stopped when he saw the city of Jerusalem. He would have had a good view of the city—of the temple and the buildings surrounding it. But Jesus didn't see the city as a group of buildings. He saw instead the issues confronting the city and those who lived there; the evil and the rejection he was to endure and the city's rejection of God. He goes into Jerusalem to the temple and drives out those who were trading there.

Think of a town or city you know well, where you live or nearby.

Imagine going somewhere where you can overlook the city—a tall building or a hill, for example. Gaze on the city, and see the landmarks and places that are important to you. Tell God about the places where you think his healing touch is needed. Where do you think his peace is needed? Where is his presence felt strongly?

Ask God to help you to begin to see the city through his eyes. What are the important places to him? Where is he loved? Where is he hated? Which parts of your city does Jesus weep over?

As you look at the city together, ask Jesus for his presence there. Intercede for the city and its people.

Maybe the next time you are in the city you could pray for some of these areas as you walk round or go to a place overlooking the city to pray.

The beauty of thy peace

As we pause in Lent, we turn to a hymn that invites us to pause and search for stillness. 'Dear Lord and Father of mankind' was originally a poem written against the over-emotional religiosity of the time. John Greenleaf Whittier (1807–92), its author, was a Quaker, and so yearned for Christians to find God in calm and silence.

Dear Lord and Father of mankind,
forgive our foolish ways!
Re-clothe us in our rightful mind,
in purer lives thy service find,
in deeper reverence praise,
in deeper reverence praise.

Drop thy still dews of quietness,
till all our strivings cease;
take from our souls the strain and stress,
and let our ordered lives confess
the beauty of thy peace,
the beauty of thy peace.

Read or sing the hymn slowly a few times. Which lines resonate with you most? Return to those lines and allow God to speak to you through them. Receive the insights they have to offer you.

Rest in the 'still dews of quietness' before beginning the busyness of life again. You may find yourself humming the hymn during the days ahead; if you do, use it as a reminder of God's work in you and his offering of himself for you.

Lent: L...E...N...T

Dorinda Miller

Love

When I hear or read the word 'Lent', it usually triggers childhood memories of being told that we were giving up sweets until Easter, because it was now Lent! It was only when I discovered faith as an adult that I came to understand the meaning and importance of Lent and its significance within the Church calendar. While there are many approaches to observing Lent and various topics that are highlighted during this season, over the next two weeks we will take a different route, looking together at three topics for each letter of the word Lent. We will begin with Love, Life, Learn, then move on to Everywhere, Explain, Expectation, followed by Now, New, Nations and ending with Time, Tenacity, Treasure.

In his first letter to the Corinthians, Paul wrote the classic Bible passage on love. In *THE MESSAGE* version, 1 Corinthians 13:4–8a, we read:

> *Love never gives up.*
> *Love cares more for others than for self.*
> *Love doesn't want what it doesn't have.*
> *Love doesn't strut,*
> *Doesn't have a swelled head,*
> *Doesn't force itself on others,*
> *Isn't always 'me first',*
> *Doesn't fly off the handle,*

Doesn't keep score of the sins of others,
Doesn't revel when others grovel,
Takes pleasure in the flowering of truth,
Puts up with anything,
Trusts God always,
Always looks for the best,
Never looks back,
But keeps going to the end.
Love never dies.

I would like to suggest that you begin this series by considering all the ways you have known God's love. Recall all the people God has placed in your life who have been channels of God's love to you, and be thankful.

Move on now to reflecting on how you feel you are doing with love at the moment by recording your thoughts and reflections as you ponder your current relationships and circumstances.

Now lay your journal aside and read the above passage slowly three times (or you may prefer to read it in another Bible version) and choose a line or two to meditate on, turning it over and over in your mind and seeing what God would say to you through it.

You may like to record these insights in your journal. Then turn the insights you receive into prayers and actions.

Life

How can we describe the journey of life? It is often like a rollercoaster: a challenging, exhilarating ride! It can be fast and frenetic, busy or boring, stressful or sedentary, or calm and peaceful.

Or perhaps life is like an onion. We have many layers to our lives, and as we journey, we often erect facades to defend or protect ourselves from the world around us. We may be unaware of these, and some of them may have their origin in events from our childhood.

We are going to consider our lives and the life of Jesus through a timeline activity, presenting a variety of events in chronological order.

Begin by looking through the Gospels and plotting on the timeline the key events in the life of Jesus. For example, his birth, his presentation at the temple, visiting the temple when he was twelve, his baptism, events in his ministry, his trial, crucifixion and resurrection.

Then draw your own timeline and plot the key events in your own life. Begin with your birth and include events up to the present time.

Now reflect on the life of Jesus and on your own life as you see them plotted on the timelines. What strikes you about his life as compared to yours in terms of lifestyle, personal qualities and relationships? What can you take from his example and apply to yourself?

End with a time of thanksgiving for God's provision, protection and blessing on your life.

Learn

Learning is a lifelong process, and there is always something new to learn if we are open to doing so.

Today I would like to encourage you to reflect on the past year and record in your journal, if you use one, what you have learnt about love, life and living for Christ over the past twelve months.

When you have done so, take a few minutes to listen to what God is saying to you about your reflections.

In order to keep growing and learning, are there any areas that you would like to develop further? What actions or strategies could you put into place to achieve this?

Read the following verses and choose one to take with you into today. Repeat it to yourself at intervals during the day—for example, as you are driving, walking or carrying out everyday tasks. Let the words sink into your heart and encourage, bless and strengthen you. You may like to write out your chosen verse on paper and add any pictures or symbols that you feel are appropriate.

> 'Are you tired? Worn out? Burned out on religion? Come to me. Get away with me and you'll recover your life. I'll show you how to take a real rest. Walk with me and work with me—watch how I do it. Learn the unforced rhythms of grace. I won't lay anything heavy or ill-fitting on you. Keep company with me and you'll learn to live freely and lightly.'
> MATTHEW 11:28–30

> So my dear friends listen carefully;
> Those who embrace these my ways are most blessed.
> Mark a life of discipline and live wisely;
> Don't squander your precious life.
> Blessed the man, blessed the woman who listens to me,
> Awake and ready for me each morning,
> Alert and responsive as I start my day's work.
> When you find me, you find life, real life,
> To say nothing of God's good pleasure.
> PROVERBS 8:32–35

Everywhere

At this time of year, as winter moves into spring, we begin to see new signs of life around us, in gardens and hedgerows, pastures and parks, woods and forests. Today I would like to suggest that you go for a walk in a park or in the countryside and look specifically for signs of growth and new life emerging from winter.

Take time to observe the barren and seemingly dead aspects of the landscape in which you are walking. What is God saying to you through these?

Reflect on your life and acknowledge any areas that you feel are barren and seemingly lifeless. Pray about these as you walk.

Take time to observe all the different signs of new life in the landscape where you are walking. What is God saying to you through these?

Reflect on your life and acknowledge any areas that you feel are developing and showing signs of new beginnings. Pray about these as you walk and give thanks to God for them.

Jesus said, 'I have come that they may have life, and have it to the full' (John 10:10, NIV 1984).

Explain

In October 2012 I attended a seminar on evangelism given by J. John and his associate Tim Saiet. Tim asked us if we could explain the hope we have in Christ: 'Always be prepared to give an answer to everyone who asks you to give a reason for the hope that you have' (1 Peter 3:15), or, as THE MESSAGE says, 'Be ready to speak up and tell anyone who asks why you are living the way you are.' He invited participants to volunteer to come up to the front and do so, within a two-minute time limit. The man Tim chose gave a brilliant response in just over two minutes! This challenged me to think carefully about how I myself would explain the hope that I have. For we do have good news to tell, and while we are not all called to be like Billy Graham or J. John, we do each have a story to tell of God's goodness and blessing in our lives.

It may be that you have already considered this and have a clear, concise way to explain the hope that you have. If so, lay it before the Lord and review it with him. If not, then think about what you would say. Prepare a two-minute answer and pray for the opportunity to 'speak up and tell anyone'.

With whom is God asking you to share the gospel during this season of Lent? Listen for names and then pray for these people. Pray for opportunities to meet them, pray for the words to say to them when you meet and pray that in the busyness of daily life you will not miss the opportunities that God gives you.

Expectations

When the women came with burial spices, at the crack of dawn on Sunday after the crucifixion of Jesus on Friday, they were expecting to find his body in the tomb. In Mark's Gospel we read that they expected the stone to be in front of the tomb and were worrying about who would roll it back for them. They were not expecting the tomb to be open, Jesus' body gone and two men with light cascading over them, asking why they were looking for the living among the dead.

Read Luke 24:1–12 and then enter into the meditation, pondering on the events and on what God might want to say to you about your own expectations at this point of your journey.

Imagine that you are with the women (or even that you are one of them) as they walk to the tomb. Take time to notice the surroundings, the buildings, the weather, the temperature, what the women are wearing.

Are they silent as they walk, or are they talking? If they are talking to each other, what are they saying? How are they feeling? Do they speak to you? How do you respond?

They reach the tomb. The stone has been rolled away! How do they react? Who goes into the tomb? They are puzzled. How do you feel?

Suddenly, seemingly out of nowhere, two men with light cascading over them appear. How do the women respond? Observe them bow in worship. Hear the men say, 'Why are you looking for the Living One in a cemetery? He is not here, but raised up. Remember how he told you when you were still back in Galilee that he had to be handed over to sinners, be killed on a cross, and in three days rise up?' (Luke 24:5–7,

THE MESSAGE). Notice how the women react to this.

As the women return to where they are staying, how are they feeling? What is going through your mind as you journey with them?

The women tell the news to the eleven. Watch as the men disbelieve them. How do they respond? Notice your own reaction and feelings. Peter, however, jumps up and goes to see for himself.

Hold these events in your mind, and in the stillness ask the Lord to reveal to you his perspective on them.

Now consider your own life. Have you experienced challenges and disappointments over your own levels of expectation? Lay these at the foot of the cross and listen to what the Lord says to you about them.

While our own expectations of people, events and circumstances may not always turn out as we would want, we can be confident in our expectation that God is faithful and always loving towards us.

You may like to end by reflecting on one of the verses below.

> *'I alone know the plans I have for you, plans to bring*
> *prosperity and not disaster, plans to bring about the future*
> *you hope for... You will pray to me, and I will answer you.'*
> JEREMIAH 29:11–12, GNB

> *Trust the Lord with all your heart. Never rely on what you*
> *think you know.*
> PROVERBS 3:5

Now

Wherever we are in our walk with God, we can always benefit from endeavouring to deepen our relationship with him and to invite him to come closer to us. In the Old Testament, the prophet Hosea wrote the following words.

> *Sow for yourselves righteousness, reap the fruit of unfailing love, and break up your unploughed ground; for it is time to seek the Lord, until he comes and showers righteousness on you.*
> HOSEA 10:12, NIV 1984

As you journey through this season of Lent, where are you now on the journey?

How are you feeling about yourself, your family and friends, your occupation, your community and your country? Record your thoughts and feelings in your journal or in some other way.

What are you thankful for in each of the above categories?

What can you praise God for in each of the above categories?

What concerns do you have for each category?

Then, just as Hezekiah spread out his letter before the Lord (2 Kings 19:14), lay out your concerns before the Lord and ask him what he wants to say or reveal to you about each of them. Then pray for each category in the light of what you have received from God.

Now, as you leave your thoughts and feelings, thanksgiving and praise and prayers safely in the hands of God, ponder these words from Mother Teresa:

> **Yesterday is gone. Tomorrow has not yet come. We have only today. Let's begin.**
> *IN THE HEART OF GOD,* NEW WORLD LIBRARY, 1997, P. 17

New

As we consider who we are, where we are, how we are, and seek to deepen and refine our faith and hope and trust in God, let us not lose sight of our ultimate destination.

In his letter to the Philippians, Paul encourages us to forget what is behind us and to strain towards what lies ahead of us: 'I press on towards the goal to win the prize for which God has called me heavenwards in Christ Jesus' (Philippians 3:14).

Slowly read the passage from Revelation below a couple of times.

Then I saw a new heaven and a new earth, for the first heaven and the first earth had passed away, and there was no longer any sea. I saw the Holy City, the new Jerusalem, coming down out of heaven from God, prepared as a bride beautifully dressed for her husband. And I heard a loud voice from the throne saying, 'Now the dwelling of God is with men, and he will live with them. They will be his people, and God himself will be with them and be their God. He will wipe every tear from their eyes. There will be no more death or mourning or crying or pain, for the old order of things has passed away.' He who was seated on the throne said, 'I am making everything new!'

REVELATION 21:1–5

Now picture this scene in your imagination.

See the new heaven and earth. Observe what they look like. Marvel at these new creations. Think about what it will be like for God to live with humans. For there to be no more death or crying or pain.

You may like to draw or paint the scene that you have just pictured. If so, take your time and allow your creative skills to flow. As you draw or paint, listen to what God is saying to you through your creation. Don't worry about the final result; there will be no public viewing.

Then reflect on the verse, 'I am making everything new.'

Finally, spend a few minutes in praise and thanksgiving to God.

Nations

We will take time today to look beyond our own personal Lenten journey to wider global issues, to pray for them and maybe even to be prompted to take specific action.

A few years ago I had the privilege of going on a number of prayer trips to the Middle East. The first one will always stand out for me as one of the most memorable weeks of my life! There were seven members of the team; we were a disparate group and most of us had hardly known each other before the trip. Yet, as we worshipped together, travelled round the country we were visiting and prayed over cities and sites, a deep unity and bond developed between us. While our hosts, who lived in the country, gave us background information at each place we visited, we took time to listen to God and to pray on our own before coming back to the group to share our insights and to pray together. The impact of these trips on the team members was significant and some of them are now themselves living and serving the Lord overseas.

In the training and orientation that we received before these trips, we were encouraged to remember six key points that are on God's heart when it comes to praying for all nations and to focus on them as we prayer-walked, namely, the glory of God (Habakkuk 2:14), hearts and minds (2 Corinthians 4:4), authority (Matthew 18:18), expansion of the kingdom (Isaiah 9:7), prosperity (Jeremiah 29:7) and revival (Luke 10:2).

In view of the events in recent years in the Middle East, perhaps you could choose one of the nations in this region to pray for. Current information can be found on the BBC World website (www.bbc.co.uk/news/world), and www.cryoutnow.org will have more information on how to pray for Syria, Lebanon, Iraq and Jordan.

Time

Time, like air, is free, and it is something of which we all have an equal amount—there are only 24 hours in a day, even if some people would prefer there to be 25, in order to get everything accomplished!

Today is an opportunity to consider our use of time and to look at some Bible verses concerning time to see how we can apply them to our current circumstances. We will also look at how we can spend some time that will be of benefit to others rather than to ourselves.

Sit in a comfortable position, close your eyes and begin by taking a deep breath in and then letting it out slowly. Do this five times.

Now, in your mind replay the past 24 hours in reverse order, beginning with sitting down, just now, and rewinding the events that preceded that, until you come to the same time yesterday. You do not need to analyse the events, just observe them.

Then think back over the past week, again in reverse order, and look at how you spent your time. How was your time apportioned?

Which activities took up most of your time?

Which activities did you spend least time on?

How do you make time for God, time for yourself, and time for others?

If you had not had the constraints of your current pattern of life, would you have made any changes to how you spent your time?

In the stillness, ask the Lord for his perspective on your use of time and record his insights in your journal. Then pray about the insights he gave you.

Read Ecclesiastes 3:1–8 three times and choose a line or two to meditate on. Turn your chosen line over and over in your mind and listen to what the Lord reveals to you.

Ephesians 2:10 tells us that 'we are God's workmanship, created in Christ Jesus to do good works, which God prepared in advance for us to do'. Can you, during this season of Lent, make time to do some acts of kindness for those with whom you come into contact during the course of the week? Those of you who enjoy using your creative skills may like to make something for a friend or relative as a gift for Easter. Allow both the creative process and the giving to be part of your prayer during this season of Lent.

A final thought:

A time to reach the poor.

A time to preach the Gospel.

The time is now!

Tenacity

'Tenacity' is defined in the Collins dictionary as being 'very determined or stubborn: tending to stick firmly to any plan, decision or opinion without changing or doubting it. Tightly held—difficult to loose, shake off or pull away from.'

In his book *Rousing the Warriors*, Steve Uppal writes:

> If the Lord has said something to you, then hold on to it despite what circumstances and other people say. We need to be tenacious about our lives, families and our churches. We also need to be tenacious about our calling and the mandate that has been given to us from the Lord. He would not call you to do something that you were unable to accomplish. He would not give you a charge and then encourage you to stop halfway.
>
> STEVE UPPAL, *ROUSING THE WARRIORS*, NEW WINE PRESS, 2008, PP. 96–97

In Proverbs 29:18a we read, 'Where there is no vision the people perish' (KJV).

Do you have a vision from the Lord for your life?

Are you clear what your particular calling is?

How tenacious are you in fulfilling this vision or calling?

Are you tenacious in prayer?

In friendships?

In the roles and responsibilities you currently find yourself in?

Record your responses in your journal.

Now choose one Old Testament character and one New Testament character who demonstrate tenacity in their calling and leadership. Read their stories, learn from them, and let them encourage you to develop and maintain tenacity.

Jesus says, 'Ask and it will be given to you; seek and you will find; knock and the door will be opened to you. For everyone who asks receives, he who seeks finds and to him who knocks the door will be opened' (Luke 11:9–10, NIV 1984).

Treasure

Most of us will have experienced losing something that we have treasured. Sometimes we do not realise that we have lost it until we come to use it. This applies not only to physical things but also to aspects of our spiritual life. For example, we may believe that silence and solitude are important for our spiritual well-being, and yet we can allow tasks and activities to overtake us until there is no time left for them. Furthermore, we can become so accustomed to our pace of life that we no longer notice that times of solitude have departed from our schedule.

In the Gospels there are accounts of lost 'treasure' being found— the woman who finds her coin, the shepherd who finds his lost sheep, the prodigal son returning to his father (see Luke 15). There are also accounts of people searching for what they needed and Jesus ministering to them and restoring their health, sight, speech and sanity.

As we reflect on our lives during this season of Lent, let us consider what 'treasure' we may have lost from our interior lives and which spiritual disciplines we could use to help us to find our lost 'treasures'.

More recently, the activity of 'treasure hunting' has been developed and used by some churches to show God's love and healing in the community (outside of the church building), predominantly with those who have not yet encountered Jesus. It is a form of evangelism in which believers go out into the community to find and bless the people God has prepared for them to meet through words of knowledge (1 Corinthians 12:8).

Kevin Dedmon's book describes how to conduct treasure hunts and has many amazing examples of how God has touched people (*The Ultimate Treasure Hunt*, Destiny Image, 2007), and the film *Father of Lights* by Darren Wilson also shows examples from around the world (Wanderlust Productions, 2012).

You may like to look into this further, through these resources, and then go on a 'treasure hunt' with some friends.

The emotions of Easter

Claire Musters

Bible reading: John 17

Start by reading this passage in order to set the scene for the coming days. It shows Jesus in prayer; praying for God to glorify him, so that he can glorify the Father by making the ultimate sacrifice. He prays in turn for himself, for his disciples and for all believers. This passage sums up the significance of his ministry. As you read it, bear in mind that Jesus is about to be arrested and tested beyond all human endurance. What does it reveal to you about Jesus, his ministry and his relationship with his followers?

Over the next two weeks we are going to be focusing on the events leading up to the cross, through Jesus' sacrifice to his victory. This period covers huge emotions—great highs and desperate lows—so we need to try to enter the story and engage with these emotions. We know the story so well that often it can lose its impact on us, but this year let us focus on understanding the cost of Jesus' sacrifice, the bewilderment of his followers, and then their tremendous joy.

Jesus washing his disciples' feet

In John 13:1–17 Jesus demonstrates the ultimate servant heart. Knowing that he is about to face the cross, he is concerned with showing his disciples how much he loves them. Read through the passage and then sit back, close your eyes and ask God to help you imagine yourself as one of the disciples at that meal.

How do you feel as Jesus starts taking off his outer garments and wraps the towel around his waist? Watch as he starts pouring the water into a basin. Do you respond like Peter ('Surely not, Jesus!')? Why would Jesus stoop to such a lowly act? But he looks at you with eyes full of such compassion, such love that, while confused, you know you can't refuse your precious friend.

Is it awkward? Your feet are caked in mud, straw and excrement; do you wince as he touches them? How does it feel as he begins to wash them clean? And how are you left feeling when he's finished with your feet and moves on to the next person? Did he look at you? Allow his love not only to touch your feet but to permeate the whole of you.

When Jesus has finished washing his followers' feet, he calls you over. Spend time talking with him and thanking him. In the closeness of the encounter, be totally honest with him about how you feel. He stooped low to wash your feet clean. What else might he do for you?

A meal with Jesus

Mark 14:12–26

Here Jesus directs his disciples to the place in which they will share a Passover meal together, instigating the first Lord's Supper, which Christians now celebrate regularly.

Having the meal that Jesus and his disciples were about to eat was something that Jews had been doing for 1500 years, ever since that first Passover. Remember, the people of Israel were slaves in Egypt. Despite numerous plagues sent to convince Pharaoh to let God's people go, his heart was still hardened—so finally God swept through Egypt, taking the life of every firstborn *except* from those who, under his direction, had sacrificed a spotless lamb and placed its blood on the tops and sides of their door frames. When God saw the blood, he would literally 'pass over' that particular house.

It was this event that finally changed Pharaoh's mind, and so the Passover meal became a symbol of sacrifice and salvation for the people of God (see Exodus 12). It was a reminder of a real historical event. But in the middle of his Passover meal, Jesus announces that soon he will become that sacrificial lamb—only this will be the once-and-for-all sacrifice! In effect, he is telling them that he is the fulfilment of all the Passover meals they have ever eaten.

For us today, Communion is so much more than just a mental exercise of remembering—it is an act of worship. It is also a symbol of Jesus' friendship with us. Jesus ate many meals with his friends. It is only in our Western culture that mealtimes have become rushed and fragmented; in many other parts of the world, meals are still an important way of building relationships. Today, Jesus offers this opportunity to you. He is inviting you to share a meal with him, so why not take some bread and wine or fruit drink, find a quiet spot and then break the bread and receive it as if he were passing it to you? Enter into the moment and share it with Jesus.

Imagine that he is saying to you, 'Take it; this is my body,' and, 'This is my blood of the covenant, which is poured out for many.' How does it feel to take it from his hands? Spend time in quiet meditation.

Looking at loneliness

In Matthew 26, Mark 14 and Luke 22, we have similar accounts of Jesus in the garden of Gethsemane. His heart is heavy; he describes it as 'overwhelmed with sorrow' (see Matthew 26:38; Mark 14:34, NIV). He needs some time with his Father, but also wants his friends to stay nearby.

Just imagine the intensity of emotions that Jesus is wrestling with at this point. They reach their peak where he cries out, 'Abba, Father… everything is possible for you. Take this cup from me' (Mark 14:36). There is a sense of panic in the human voice, and yet his being submits: 'yet not my will, but yours be done' (Luke 22:42). Luke's account indicates that once he submitted in this way, an angel appeared and 'strengthened' him (v. 43). But, even after this visitation, the anguish was still upon him, his prayer intensified and his sweat became like 'drops of blood' (v. 44).

Matthew's account reveals how Jesus went back to his friends, presumably for support and to check that they were praying for him. Three times he went to them, and each time he found them asleep. Perhaps they hadn't grasped the enormity of the situation; certainly they allowed tiredness to overcome them. He must have felt so alone.

We can't begin to compare our own situations with Jesus', but there are times when we are overwhelmed with loneliness, sadness and despair. Perhaps your friends have let you down by not doing something or by acting in a way that has hurt you. Perhaps God is asking you to face a situation you feel is too difficult; why would he ask it of you? How do you respond—to your friends, and to God? In the garden, Jesus is modelling the most helpful response: pour it all out to God in prayer: the hurt, despair, pain, sadness. Jesus ends with, 'Rise, let us go!' (Mark 14:42). He uses his time in prayer to be real about his emotional struggle, and then meets the situation head on.

If you have been hurt, it can be helpful to write a letter (to God or as if to the person involved). Express all your emotions as you do this.

Sometimes it will be necessary to speak to the person, in which case the letter can be a good way to express the intensity of your feelings before working out the best way to approach a meeting with grace. At other times, it is simply right to bring the letter before God, read it out and then tear it up, asking him to take away the pain as you do so, or to give you the strength to face the difficult situation.

Did you disown him?

Luke 22:54–62

Shortly before the events in this passage, Jesus had told Peter that he would disown him, and Peter had vehemently denied it. But just think of the confusion that the disciples must have felt. Even though Jesus had explained what would happen, they still couldn't understand it. Peter tried to stop one guard by cutting off his ear, and then followed at a distance. Where were all the others? Had they sloped off, fearing for their lives and disappointed that Jesus had given in? Peter was still around, surely showing some solidarity. However, when challenged directly, look how he answers, each time trying to distance himself from Jesus: 'Woman, I don't know him,' 'Man, I am not!' and 'Man, I don't know what you are talking about!' And then Jesus looks straight at him. How ashamed Peter must have felt!

Before you condemn Peter, though, and indeed all the other disciples, try putting yourself in their shoes. What would you have done? Do you think you would have fled when Jesus was arrested? Perhaps you would have followed to see what would happen to him. How would you have answered if you were directly challenged as Peter was? Now, let's turn this into a situation relevant for today: what do you do when faced with situations that should result in your standing up against the cultural tide? Have you ever thought that, by staying silent, or by denying your faith, you are disowning him?

Spend some time praying for the situations and people that you face on a daily basis. Ask God for the courage to be his ambassador.

Suffering servant

Jesus conquered death to rise again, fully victorious. But do we really understand what his human body had to go through in order to accomplish this? There isn't much detail within the Gospels, presumably because crucifixion was such a common form of execution at that time, and as readers today we can perhaps gloss over the horror. Rather than recoiling from the facts below, ask God to allow the truth to penetrate and soften your heart. Remember: Jesus went through all this for you.

- Crucifixion was vindictively cruel, lasting for several hours to ensure that the torture was as barbaric as possible. The victim was crucified naked and placed high above ground so that as many people as possible could see them.
- The condemned person had to carry their own cross to the place of crucifixion. It would probably have been the cross arm that was carried, as the uprights were usually already in place (and were reused). This cross arm would still have been about seven to eight feet long, one foot wide, weighing at least 100 pounds. The wood would have been splintered and rough.
- Jesus would have been a strong man as his work as a carpenter was very physical, so his need for help with the cross was probably due to the scourging he endured first. He would have lost an immense amount of blood as they beat him with whips made of strips of leather that contained small balls of lead at either end. These would first rip the skin, and then tear the flesh right down to the muscle until his back was a mass of hanging ribbons of flesh.
- The Romans placed a crown of thorns on him, which scholars agree

would have been made up of one to two inch thorns so hard that they would probably have penetrated his skull and caused haemorrhaging. The robe they dressed him in to mock him was then ripped back off him, causing extra bleeding and pain.

- Jesus was then laid down on the cross and nails were banged into his wrists and feet. These would have been like long garden spikes, heavy and square, about six to eight inches long. When hammered into the feet, the Romans would bend the knees of the victim, which forced him to push his body up to breathe, causing excruciating pain.

- A plaque with 'King of the Jews' was placed on the cross and Jesus was mocked, spat upon and his beard plucked out. He hung there for six hours, feeling utter separation from his Father, until finally the body's dehydrated tissue became too dry and his lungs asphyxiated. Jesus simply said, 'It is finished' before committing his spirit into his Father's hands.

- To make sure that the victims were dead before sundown, the Roman guards broke their legs; but they didn't need to do this to Jesus. They did test that he was dead by driving a lance through his side. Physicians take John's description in his Gospel of 'a sudden flow of blood and water' (John 19:34) to mean that the water fluid from the sac around the heart escaped, revealing that he actually died of heart failure.

We have no idea, also, what intense spiritual attack may have been launched on him during the crucifixion. But surely we can never again say that Jesus doesn't understand our suffering. He is more than able to empathise and support us in our personal experiences. Why not spend some time thanking him for suffering for you, and asking him to help you bear whatever you are going through?

Meditation

Sit in a comfortable position, still your mind and slowly read through the meditation below. The parts are spoken by different characters, so mull them over carefully. Try to use it to picture what was going on. Let your imagination fill in the blanks until you clearly see the scenes. With whom do you empathise most?

'What was that all about? What has just happened? I don't understand—how can they justify this?'

'Did you see the marks on his back, the deep grooves gushing with blood? I could hardly look at him. How could they do this? I thought he was our saviour—our king. How could he keep silent when they mocked him?'

'Oh God, why? He's my precious one, my baby. I thought he was your precious one too. Why are you letting them do this to him? How could you? Why did you pick me? I'm not strong enough for this. I don't think I can watch anymore. Are you really in control?'

'Wow, this cross is heavy, and that guy looks in a really bad way already. What have they done to him? And what has he done to deserve this?'

'Oh my son, my son. What have they done to you? This is so hard to bear. Not to interfere. But there isn't long to go now. My heart is breaking—but I am so, so proud of you.'

'We've done it! And look—he really is just a man. He was supposed to be their king, but he hasn't been able to save himself. How pathetic! Come down and show us who you are! No? Can't do it? Didn't think so.'

'Oh God, I don't think I can keep going for much longer. Are you there? Abba, where are you?'

'You haven't done anything wrong, have you? I can see it just by looking at you. Please remember me—I long for a second chance.'

'Mother... dear friend... love one another, care for one another.'

'Mary, he's seen you. Mary, try and stand. Try and be there for him—he needs you more than ever.'

'My God, my God, please don't leave me! Why have you forsaken me?... It is finished! Father, receive my spirit...'

'Surely he was the son of God!'

'That was strange. Kind of eerie. I'm not sticking around here. We've done our job—let's go!'

'I'm not leaving his body there. I don't trust them. I'm going to Pilate to ask for his body. He needs—he deserves—a proper resting place.'

'Oh Mary, I'm so sorry. I don't know what to say. But I think we should follow this man—let's see where he takes him. Come, hold on to my arm...'

Empty?

Spend some time meditating on these words from a well-known hymn:

> Thine be the glory, risen, conqu'ring Son;
> Endless is the victory thou o'er death hast won;
> Angels in bright raiment rolled the stone away,
> Kept the folded grave clothes where thy body lay.
>
> Lo! Jesus meets us, risen from the tomb;
> Lovingly he greets us, scatters fear and gloom;
> Let the church with gladness, hymns of triumph sing;
> For her Lord now liveth, death hath lost its sting.
>
> WORDS BY EDMOND BUDRY (1854–1932), TRANSLATED BY RICHARD HOYLE
> (1875–1939)

Read Matthew 28:1–8, and try to put yourself in Mary's shoes. How might you have felt arriving at the tomb only to be greeted by an earthquake and then a terrifying angel? The angel then actually *speaks* to you, telling you that Jesus is alive and that you are to spread the news! Well, how would you feel? Petrified? Unbelieving at first, but with faith rising in you that perhaps this is what Jesus had meant all along? What a confusing mass of information, but perhaps, just perhaps, it is all true...

Take the muddle of emotions and thoughts in your head now and put something down on paper. You could try writing a poem or song lyrics that focus on Mary's emotions.

Celebrate—he's alive!

Whether you are musical or not, there must be times when you enjoy a party. What better reason to celebrate than the news of Jesus' resurrection? Reflect on that amazing news and allow your emotions to bubble up and outwards. Get hold of whatever instruments you have in your home and use them to explore your response to the resurrection; let the music you make echo feelings of joy and amazement.

If you find it difficult to express yourself without singing a song, you could use the following modern hymn, written by David Grieve. It is sung to the tune of 'Morning has broken':

> *Christ is arisen!*
> *New day is dawning,*
> *Sin and death conquered,*
> *No more to reign.*
> *Christ is arisen!*
> *Praise to the highest!*
> *Let us adore him,*
> *Mighty to save.*
>
> *Christ is arisen!*
> *We are arisen,*
> *Sharing in new life*
> *That never ends.*
> *Christ is arisen!*
> *Lord of all glory*
> *Calls us to serve him,*
> *Spread the Good News.*
>
> *Christ is arisen!*
> *He sends God's Spirit,*
> *Holy and humble,*

Loving and true.
Christ is arisen!
With us forever.
Let us be faithful
Right to the end.
© DAVID GRIEVE

Don't doubt—believe!

Do you sometimes find it hard to believe the events of the first Easter? If you ever have moments of doubt, then ask God to use this reflection on what may have been going on in doubting Thomas' mind to flood your heart with the truth (see John 20).

'What are those women talking about? Why on earth, if Jesus really was alive—and I'm certainly not saying he is—would he appear to them? They must be deluded. They've probably allowed their grief to take over and imagined he appeared before them. I know Peter said that he went into the tomb and saw the strips of linen and nothing else. But the guards could have just moved Jesus' body. A sensible security measure, if you ask me. I can't believe Peter is entertaining these women's stories!

'Wait a minute. What's going on? Why are the other disciples now saying that they have seen him alive? Why would he do that—come to them and not me? They must be as deluded as those silly women. I know I upset them by reminding them of what he went through, but I'm not sorry I said that I wouldn't believe until I saw him for myself and put my fingers where the nails pierced him. That shut them up. I'm getting sick and tired of hearing about this. The whole thing is ridiculous.

'... Oh Jesus, is that really you? Jesus, I am so sorry—you are my God, my king. Yes, I feel those nail holes, I will touch your broken side, even though I no longer need to do so. You went through that for me? I am so sorry I ever doubted.

'I really wanted to spend more time with him, but Jesus had to go. He said that I had believed because I saw him, but that others would believe without seeing him. That's what we are to do: tell others about him and what he's done. All that time we spent with him was to prepare us for this moment.

'It's funny how all the pieces seem to fit together. Such as the way he allowed them to lead him to the cross; he really was like the Passover lamb. I'm still trying to understand, but I no longer doubt. I believe, and am determined to do what he asked me to. I'm not going to let him down again.'

Reflections on the cross

Make a cross out of paper and write on it all that the cross means to you, perhaps using words such as 'salvation', 'love' or 'freedom'. Make it personal to your experiences and situation. Then, using those words, create a piece of artwork. You may want simply to paint the cross and words, or create a collage in the shape of the cross. As you are creating, meditate one by one on the words that you wrote down. When you have finished, spend time using the artwork as a basis for prayer, responding to how you felt when you were making it. Thank Jesus for what he accomplished on the cross *for you*.

Focus on a chosen part or word for the rest of the day as an act of worship.

Come back to your artwork daily.

Empowered from on high

Do you live in the light of Jesus' resurrection? Does it impact what you do, how you live, and the decisions you make? The New Testament is full of information about our inheritance in Christ. Read Colossians 1. Verses 15 to 20 list Jesus' credentials, proving his utter supremacy. Note that 'God was pleased to… reconcile to himself all things… by making peace through his blood, shed on the cross' (vv. 19–20). And in 2:9–15 we have our relationship to him spelt out. We have been given fullness in Christ (v. 10). God cancelled our judgment, nailing it to the cross, and Jesus 'disarmed the powers and authorities [and] made a public spectacle of them, triumphing over them by the cross' (v. 15). We have focused on what he suffered physically, but now we read how he defeated our enemy forever. Allow faith and thankfulness to God to rise up in your heart.

The next chapter of Colossians charges us with what our response should be. Knowing that our lives are now 'hidden with Christ in God' (3:3), we should purposefully 'set [our] minds on things above, not on earthly things' (v. 2). We are told to put to death all sin and live a life of love and peace. Read through this chapter, not with a heavy heart, looking at a list of rules, but as one enjoying freedom and power that was bought for you at a hefty cost. Jesus is the one who enables you to live a life worthy of him; it isn't all up to you.

Here are some practical ideas for how to keep these things in mind daily.

It is interesting to note the wording of verse 12 here: 'clothe yourselves with compassion, kindness, humility, gentleness and patience' [my emphasis]. Have you ever thought of clothing your spirit or character in the same way as you cover your body? Why not ask God when you are getting dressed to help you put on each of these qualities, and to remind you of them during the day? Remember, for example, that you are wearing a garment of patience, so respond patiently to those around you!

Try creating a bookmark or mini fridge poster with scriptures that help to remind you of what Jesus has done for you, your standing in Christ, and how you should live as a result. Philippians 2 is a good place to start, if you need an example.

Take time out to meditate on particular scriptures at various times of the day. Write them out or put them on your phone and set an alarm reminder so that you remember to look at them.

Journalling

Sally Smith

In *Quiet Spaces* you will often read something about writing what you have been praying in your journal. For some readers, this will be the most natural thing in the world to do at that point in a prayer session. For others, it might seem a strange thing to do, and you might have some questions about this practice. I have been keeping a prayer journal for most of my adult life. I can see a pile of them sitting on a shelf in my study, and although I rarely look inside them, I know that within those covers there is a wealth of experience and spiritual development, of real gems and also of total rubbish, things I would be amazed to find I had written and things I might even be ashamed to have written.

If I were to sit and read my journals, I would see the prayer journey I have been on for those years. I would see the highs and the lows, and would be encouraged by some of the things that happened. I would find promises God has kept and be surprised by how important some issues seemed at the time. I would also see how I have grown and developed over the years, seeing the points of revelation and the slow formation of the person God is making me. There are the times I have praised God and the times I have shouted at him in anger or frustration. There is healing and there is encounter with God.

Journals, as you would expect, are very personal things. We each approach them in different ways and will perceive different benefits from keeping one. The act of journalling goes beyond simply keeping a journal. To keep a journal is to keep a record of what has been happening, maybe to reflect upon those events. To journal is to allow the Holy Spirit into the process, to allow God to work in you as you write or draw. In journalling there is an expectation of movement within at some level, so that it becomes a place of learning about ourselves and about God in us. It allows the subconscious to be opened and hidden emotions and expressions to surface. In the journalling after a prayer session fresh images may emerge and new light may shine on our experiences.

So let me share something of what journalling has been like for me. Maybe some of you reading this will be inspired to start a journal with confidence, others may return to their neglected journals, and still others may find fresh inspiration and new approaches to an old habit.

For me it's important to have the 'right' book to write in. I know this shouldn't be important, and that it's the content and process that are important, but there is something about a nice book with an attractive cover that makes me want to use it. I need to be able to attach value to the book and through the book to the contents as well; a special book deserves special contents. I tend to use hardback books with plain pages for my spiritual journals, which allow me to draw and stick things in as well as writing, but a cheap exercise book will work just as well.

Most entries start as a record of things that have been happening in my prayer life. This might be after a prayer session on my own, as suggested in *Quiet Spaces* or during a Quiet Day or retreat. I begin by writing an account of what I did and thought, where I felt God was and what I felt God was saying to me. This can help clarify what exactly has happened, and often in the writing I remember something I might otherwise have forgotten. Knowing that I will revisit the prayer session and reflect on the process, I am then able to give everything to prayer without struggling to analyse what is happening, and leave reflecting on the experience for later. The temptation when praying can be to wonder what it's all about and to spend the time reflecting on this rather than spending the time with God, allowing him to speak, learning from him and enjoying his presence. Times with God are to be valued for what is given in that moment.

The recording of what happened is also a place for learning to notice what is happening. This time spent is valuable, going over the detail and seeing what is going on that we may not be aware of at the time—the subconscious experience. God's grace is such that he doesn't always shout out loud what he is doing; he speaks in that still small voice, and moves in quiet and mysterious ways. But by training ourselves to listen and to notice, we can see what God is doing, work with him and be thankful. It can be tempting to think that nothing is going on in a prayer session, but by allowing time for it to be revealed, and learning to listen and watch carefully, we become aware of God's presence and work.

This can all be achieved by pausing at the end of a prayer session and thinking about the experience, allowing time to reflect and for God to bring to the surface things that have been happening deep inside; remembering with pleasure God's presence and lingering on the experience. This can be over a cup of coffee or walking round the garden. Personally, I find my mind wanders if I do this, and the act of writing focuses my mind and ensures I pay full attention. In the act of writing I gain freedom to express what is hidden in ways that I can't achieve in thought.

I often find a retelling of the experience starts me off and I can then move deeper. I may write a letter to God, expressing what I am feeling, or responding to him. This can be a gentle letter of thankfulness, or, more often, a letter of anger or frustration, a shout and a rage: why did that have to happen? I want… Don't you know…? When are you going to answer? As I write, it can all pour out. Several things are happening. I am being honest with myself: all is not well and this is how I feel. I am being honest with God: I know you know, but I don't agree and I feel like this, whatever you say. I am allowing God into that deeper place where those emotions live and inviting him to share them, and in sharing them I am also inviting God to work through them and with them, not to take them away, but to mould them and cherish them in ways I can't begin to imagine.

It can equally be a love letter to God, expressing my love for him and the place he occupies in my life, reminding me of what he has given me and how much I want to give back to him.

I may then allow God to write his reply to me, for him to share his perspective and often to remind me that he still loves me, that, whatever I throw at him, he is still there and is with me in all that's going on.

Often at the start of a Quiet Day or a retreat I will draw my life, allowing colours and shapes to appear on the page and, through them, recognising where I am in different aspects of my life (spiritual, relationships, work, church...). This often brings up unexpected issues. I may be surprised at the prominence of one issue, thinking I had come with one area I wanted to sort out, and realising that the day was about to head off in a different direction. This may be God's leading me, or my discovering that my priorities are not what I had thought them to be, and that there is something hidden deeper inside that the space is allowing to surface. When drawing, it is the process that is important and the final 'artwork' is not meant for other human eyes. I will often share it with my spiritual director as a way of explaining what is happening, but the real value is in discovering more about myself and where and who God is for me at that moment. The colours and shapes I use can be revealing. Why did I use so much blue? What is that splodge of yellow? Why are there so many sharp corners? Where is God in this? Where would I like God to be? What of this do I want to share with God?

Drawing at the beginning and end of a Quiet Day can give a sense of the journey that has been undertaken during the day. What has moved? How have I moved? Where am I compared with the start of the day? Where is God now? Or I may respond to a prayer session with drawing. What colours and shapes describe the session and where I am now?

I also use my journal for praying. I might take a psalm and rewrite it, making it personal to me, including my name or circumstances. Or I may model my own psalm on one I have been using in prayer.

I have had periods when I focused on the negatives and have found it helpful at the end of each day to reflect on what good has happened during the day; what good gifts God has given to me today. After 'watching the video' of the day, for what can I be thankful? When have I encountered God? What do I want to say to God about what he has given me? These can be specific things, events, the actions of others, or emotions.

I also write down any prayers or quotations that have been particularly pertinent or powerful for me. I often then return to these over the following days, allowing them to feed me further as I draw out the goodness from them. Sometimes quotes lie dormant in my journal for a while until the right time, but then they are there ready to feed and sustain me and draw me on further.

So, I would recommend to those who have not tried journalling to give it a go. Maybe this Lent is a good time to begin. Allow it to be an adventure and see where God takes you on the journey. Be honest with yourself and with God. Try to get beyond the recording level to the feeling and response level. Explore what is happening inside. There is no 'right' way to journal, so experiment and see what helps you and what is manageable for you. Write at different times and in different places. Draw, stick in pictures, photos, leaves, newspaper cuttings... anything that draws you closer to God and deeper into yourself. Above all, enjoy it; allow your journal to become your friend.

Of course there are many other ways of recording your experiences and exploring them further, so when you see the words 'record it in your journal', do feel free to respond as appropriate for you at that time.

As a Child

Phil Steer

Childish

> *When I was a child, I talked like a child, I thought like a child,*
> *I reasoned like a child. When I became a man, I put* childish
> *ways behind me.*
> 1 CORINTHIANS 13:11, NIV 1984, EMPHASIS MINE

'Oh, grow up! Act your age! Stop being so childish!' What parents have not, at some time or other, uttered exclamations such as these in utter exasperation at their child's behaviour? We are generally fairly willing to indulge childish behaviour from the very young; indeed, we might even find it rather amusing and endearing. But as our children grow older and begin to learn how they ought to behave, we find it less and less acceptable when they don't do as they should—and quite right, too!

The apostle Paul seems to echo these cries of the exasperated parent in his letters to the churches in Corinth and Ephesus: 'put childish ways behind you' (see 1 Corinthians 13:11), 'stop thinking like children' (1 Corinthians 14:20), 'no longer be infants' and 'grow up' (Ephesians 4:14–15). What could be clearer? Childhood is for children, not for adults. We are not meant to remain stuck in the patterns of thought and behaviour that characterised our early years. As we grow older we are to grow up, to develop, to mature. This is the way of things, the way that life should be.

When we think back to our children's early years, when we look at old photos and watch old home movies, we may perhaps sometimes experience a touch of nostalgic sadness. But the truth is that we wouldn't want them to stay that way for ever. For of course, there are some children who do not fully mature—be that physically, mentally, emotionally, or socially—and this can be a cause of great sadness.

But in calling for us to become like little children, Jesus is not saying that we should not grow and mature—and he is certainly not saying that we should continue in childish behaviour. His call is for us to become not child*ish* but child*like*, and there is a world of difference between the two. Indeed, sad to say, were it childish behaviour that Jesus seeks, there would be little need for him to encourage us in it, since this comes perfectly naturally to most of us.

It needs no special effort on my part to be immature, insecure, irresponsible and infantile—and I suspect that I am not alone in this. We can all be self-centred, attention-seeking and manipulative; we can all get angry and sulk if we don't get what we want. Being childish is not something that most of us lose as we grow up. We might become better at hiding such childish reactions, but that childish nature remains with us no matter how old we get.

Being childlike is something entirely different.

If we look at Paul's words in context, we see that he is in no way discouraging childlike behaviour. His comment about putting childish ways behind him occurs towards the end of his teaching about love, famous for its use in countless wedding services. Prophecies will cease, tongues will be stilled, knowledge will pass away, but love will remain. When perfection comes, the imperfect disappears. Paul is cautioning a church that has become too preoccupied with the spiritual gifts. The gifts are important, but not that important. When compared with love, they are but childish things. Ultimately they will be left behind, as all childish things must be. When God's kingdom comes in all its fullness, there will no longer be any need for spiritual gifts. They will pass, but love will remain.

Similarly, when Paul tells the church in Corinth to 'stop thinking like children', he is again concerned with their attitude to spiritual gifts (and in particular the gift of tongues). They are not to be like a child with a new toy, playing with the gifts for their own pleasure and amusement. Rather, they are to exercise the gifts with wisdom and understanding, and to seek to grow in those gifts 'that build up the church' (1 Corinthians 14:12). The gifts are given for the good of others, not to inflate our egos. Again, it is a childish attitude to the gifts— immature, self-centred and attention-seeking—that Paul is counselling against.

What, then, of Paul's instruction to the believers in Ephesus that they are to 'grow up' and 'no longer be infants'? This seems clear enough; but again, the context reveals a different story. The 'infants' that Paul refers to are those whom he characterises as being 'tossed back and forth by the waves, and blown here and there by every wind of teaching and by the cunning and craftiness of men in their deceitful scheming' (Ephesians 4:14). In other words, to be an 'infant' is to have an unsteady and uncertain faith, too easily drawn away from the truth of Christ by the lies of the world. It is being worldly, being immature in our faith, neither knowing nor living the truth of God's word. This is not the way we should be; instead, we are to grow up into Christ—into his truth, into his love, into the fullness of all that he is and all that he desires us to be.

'Put childish ways behind you', 'stop thinking like children', 'no longer be infants', 'grow up'. As we have seen, none of these statements from Paul in any way runs counter to Jesus' call for us to become more childlike. We are not to be immature in the level of our love; we are not to be immature in our use of the spiritual gifts; we are not to be immature in our understanding and practice of God's word. We are to grow out of such childish ways—but we are also to grow into the likeness of a child.

As I hope is clear, I am in no way suggesting that we should revert entirely to the attitudes and actions of childhood, rejecting all aspects of our adult life and faith. We should of course welcome and encourage the maturity, knowledge and experience that we gain as we grow into adulthood; for there are many situations and tasks and challenges that we need to approach as adults, drawing upon all the resources with which our years have endowed us.

When Jesus sent out the twelve disciples, he counselled them to be 'as shrewd as snakes and as innocent as doves' (Matthew 10:16). He was, in effect, instructing them to combine the wisdom that comes from age and experience with the simplicity of a little child; an echo of his wider call for us to live undivided lives, our adult self and our childlike self journeying together, hand in hand, united as one.

We know just what it means to live as adults; it's what we do: naturally, instinctively, for the most part unthinkingly. Our adult self assumes his or her place as of right, whilst the little child is pushed to the margins. Hence, there is little need for me to keep putting the adult perspective, to give voice to the adult whom we know so well, and who all too often dismisses and drowns out the voice of the child. My purpose, therefore, is simply to do as Jesus did: to call forward our childlike self, to bring him out of obscurity, and to place her right in the centre of what it means to live in the fullness of the kingdom of God.

Spotlight: The Ammerdown retreat and conference centre

Bénédicte Scholefield, Director

Nestling in the idyllic rolling countryside near Bath lies Ammerdown, a retreat and conference centre with a difference. It is a place for people longing for freedom to be themselves, a safe accepting space where they can rest their soul, mind and body, connect with who they really are, and be renewed.

Ammerdown was founded 40 years ago by committed Roman Catholics who responded to Vatican II and its clarion call to church members to become more involved in worldly affairs and with other faiths. The founding vision was for a place where people of different backgrounds, traditions and faiths could meet and learn from each other. This special place had to be residential because the founders knew that it was as much in fellowship over meals, sharing over a glass of wine and the walks together in the beautiful grounds that guests would encounter 'the other'. Since opening in June 1973 we have welcomed thousands of people from different faith backgrounds, and others with none, and have given them an opportunity to learn from each other.

The Centre's first director was a Methodist, establishing from the very beginning Ammerdown's intent to foster dialogue between different faith traditions. Soon afterwards a group of Sisters of Sion arrived to help run the Centre, thereby adding a Jewish Christian dimension. As years went by, dialogue with other faiths was progressively developed.

Today the Centre offers comfortable facilities in 40 en-suite bedrooms, six conference rooms, excellent food and a caring service from a dedicated team. It is run as an open Christian community, which offers, in Ammerdown's beautiful chapel, services of morning and evening prayer, to which everyone is welcome, irrespective of faith background.

Interfaith dialogue remains a central part of our work, and every year we continue to create opportunities for people of different traditions to meet or learn about other faiths. We are the only UK centre to host residential 'Three Faiths Weeks', and our annual programme is peppered with interfaith courses.

Offering a safe and accepting space to people who feel marginalised or 'second class' citizens also remains a central tenet of our work. In the mid-1980s Ammerdown was the first retreat centre to welcome HIV sufferers at the request of Rabbi Lionel Blue, who had knocked at every door he could think of and had been turned down by all... except us! Lionel's charity continues to bring its members for a weekend every year, and similarly we host a whole range of events for others who feel vulnerable or marginalised, such as those with mental illness, M.E. sufferers or exhausted carers.

Many guests comment on the distinctive Ammerdown atmosphere. They say that there is quite simply 'something in the air' that makes it special. I believe that it is to do with the spirit in which Ammerdown was created, the founding values of openness and acceptance that continue to permeate everything that Ammerdown is and does.

Feedback from guests is very important to us, and what we achieve is summed up by one who commented: 'Ammerdown is such a nurturing, inclusive place, with a deep sense of inner peace, which is perfect to rest, reflect and renew. It is not just that I was being cared for—which of course I was, in a very sensitive way—but I also felt invited in as a special guest. At Ammerdown you are made to feel like you have been invited to a feast, have been led through the doorway and given a place at the table... this gives you a special feeling of communion that goes far beyond ordinary hospitality.'

The special kind of hospitality that we aim to provide at Ammerdown was superbly put into words by Henri Nouwen in his book *Reaching Out*: 'Hospitality means primarily the creation of a free space where the stranger can enter and become a friend instead of an enemy. Hospitality is not to change people, but to offer a space where change can take place... It is not a method of making our God and our way into the criteria of happiness, but the opening to others to find their God and their way' (Fount, 1976, p. 49).

In June last year, Ammerdown celebrated its 40th anniversary. For those 40 years, Ammerdown has been a blessing to countless people, and given them an opportunity to be refreshed and renewed. My hope is that it will continue to be a blessing to those who come through its doors for many more years to come.

For more information about the Ammerdown Centre, visit www. ammerdown.org

Quiet Spaces Subscription

Please note one-year subscription prices below include postage and packing.

You can also purchase your subcription by Direct Debit. Complete the details on the direct debit form and post to BRF with the order form.

Please send *Quiet Spaces* beginning with the May 2014/September 2014/January 2015 issue (delete as applicable).

PRICES FOR UK ADDRESSES

DESCRIPTION	PRICE	QUANTITY ORDERED	TOTAL
Individual 1-year subscription Includes postage and packing	£15.99		
Group 1-year subscription Postage and packing FREE	£12.75		
ORDER TOTAL			

PRICES FOR OVERSEAS ADDRESSES

DESCRIPTION	PRICE	QUANTITY ORDERED	TOTAL
Individual 1-year subscription Airmail includes postage and packing	£25.50		
Individual 1-year subscription Surface includes postage and packing	£23.25		
ORDER TOTAL			

Prices are correct at time of going to press and subject to change. For information about group subscriptions, please contact BRF at the address given overleaf.

Method of payment

☐ Cheque ☐ MasterCard ☐ Maestro ☐ Visa ☐ Postal Order

Card no. ☐☐☐☐ ☐☐☐☐ ☐☐☐☐ ☐☐☐☐ ▨▨▨

Shaded boxes for Maestro use only

Valid from ☐☐☐☐ Expires ☐☐☐☐ Issue No. (Switch only) ☐☐☐☐

Security code* ☐☐☐ (Last 3 digits on the reverse of the card)
(*Essential in order to process your order*)

0000 **000**
EXAMPLE

Signature .... Date ...... / ...... / ....

All subscription orders must be accompanied by the appropriate payment.

Please note: do not send payments for group orders. All group orders will be invoiced.

Name ....

Acc. No. ....

Address ....

....

.... Postcode ....

Telephone ....

Email ....

BRF, 15 The Chambers, Vineyard, Abingdon OX14 3FE;
Tel: 01865 319700 Fax: 01865 319701
www.brf.org.uk email: enquiries@brf.org.uk
BRF is a registered charity (no: 233280)

BRF Quiet Days

BRF Quiet Days are an ideal way of redressing the balance in our busy lives. Held in peaceful locations around the country, each one is led by an experienced speaker and gives the opportunity to reflect, be silent and pray, and through it all to draw closer to God. The 2014 programme is as follows:

Wednesday, 19 March: 'At the End of the Day—Enjoying Life in the Departure Lounge', led by David Winter at Ivy House, St Denys Retreat Centre, Warminster, Wiltshire, BA12 8PG

Wednesday, 16 April: 'Jesus at the Hands of Others' led by Ann Persson at Jordans Quaker Centre, Jordans Meeting House, Welders Lane, Jordans, Buckinghamshire, HP9 2SN

Thursday, 1 May: 'Watch My Lips…' led by Bridget and Adrian Plass at Scargill House, nr Skipton, North Yorkshire, BD23 5HU

Thursday, 22 May: 'What kind of love is this? Living and serving as God's beloved children' led by Tony Horsfall at The Mirfield Centre, Mirfield, West Yorkshire, WF14 0BN

Wednesday, 2 July: 'Living in the Secret Place, from Psalm 91' led by Jennifer Rees Larcombe at House of Retreat, The Street, Pleshey, Chelmsford, Essex, CM3 1HA

Thursday, 10 July: '"Abba–Father"—the spirituality at the heart of the Lord's Prayer' led by Joanna Collicutt at Harnhill Centre of Christian Healing, Harnhill Manor, Cirencester, Gloucestershire, GL7 5PX

Thursday, 21 August: 'Arise, my love and come with me' led by Ann Persson at Carmelite Priory, Boars Hill, Oxford, Oxfordshire, OX1 5HB

Friday, 3 October: 'Matthew: his Master's Voice' led by David Winter at Douai Abbey, Upper Woolhampton, Reading, Berkshire, RG7 5TQ

Thursday, 27 November: 'Ray of Light: a Quiet Day for Advent' led by Ian Adams at Mill House, Rochnell Manor Farm, Westleigh, Tiverton, Devon, EX16 7ES

Monday, 1 December: 'Mary' led by Andrew Jones at Gladstone's Library, Church Lane, Hawarden, Flintshire, CH5 3DF

For further details and to book, please go to www.brfonline.org.uk/events-and-quiet-days/ or contact us at BRF, 15 The Chambers, Vineyard, Abingdon, Oxfordshire, OX14 3FE; tel: 01865 319700

Direct Debit

Now you can pay for your annual subscription to BRF notes using Direct Debit. You need only give your bank details once, and the payment is made automatically every year until you cancel it. If you would like to pay by Direct Debit, please use the form opposite, entering your BRF account number under 'Reference'.

You are fully covered by the Direct Debit Guarantee:

The Direct Debit Guarantee

DIRECT Debit

- This Guarantee is offered by all banks and building societies that accept instructions to pay Direct Debits.
- If there are any changes to the amount, date or frequency of your Direct Debit, The Bible Reading Fellowship will notify you 10 working days in advance of your account being debited or as otherwise agreed. If you request The Bible Reading Fellowship to collect a payment, confirmation of the amount and date will be given to you at the time of the request.
- If an error is made in the payment of your Direct Debit, by The Bible Reading Fellowship or your bank or building society, you are entitled to a full and immediate refund of the amount paid from your bank or building society.
  - If you receive a refund you are not entitled to, you must pay it back when The Bible Reading Fellowship asks you to.
- You can cancel a Direct Debit at any time by simply contacting your bank or building society. Written confirmation may be required. Please also notify us.

The Bible Reading Fellowship

Instruction to your bank or
building society to pay by Direct Debit

Please fill in the whole form using a ballpoint pen and send to The Bible
Reading Fellowship, 15 The Chambers, Vineyard, Abingdon OX14 3FE.

Service User Number: | 5 | 5 | 8 | 2 | 2 | 9 |

Name and full postal address of your bank or building society

To: The Manager ....

.... Bank/Building Society

Address ....

....

.... Postcode ....

Name(s) of account holder(s)

Branch sort code

☐☐ – ☐☐ – ☐☐

Bank/Building Society account no.

☐☐☐☐☐☐☐☐

Reference

☐☐☐☐☐☐☐

Instruction to your Bank/Building Society

Please pay The Bible Reading Fellowship Direct Debits from the account
detailed in this instruction, subject to the safeguards assured by the Direct
Debit Guarantee. I understand that this instruction may remain with The
Bible Reading Fellowship and, if so, details will be passed electronically to
my bank/building society.

Signature(s)

....
                                                                                          Date

Banks and Building Societies may not accept Direct Debit instructions for
some types of account.